IN LIVINGSTONE'S FOOTSTEPS

Walking the Mighty Zambezi

by
David Lemon

`

ISBN-13: 978-1540418647

ISBN-10: 1540418642

This one is for **Ronnie Henwood** and **Johan Mawaya Hougaard**
– bushmen, explorers and true friends.

Only those who will risk going too far can
possibly find out how far one can go.
T.S. Eliot.

Contents

For

Norman —

Memories of Africa

Perhaps?

4-4-17.

Acknowledgements

No journey such as the one described in these pages can be done without assistance and I was extremely fortunate with my sponsors, as well as the lovely people I met along the way.

Andy Taylor and his wonderful Cowbell team were always on hand when I needed them; Tom Naude and the cheerful staff at Fluxcon trustingly loaned me a satellite phone that ultimately saved my life and First Quantum Minerals provided the aircraft that brought me out of Mozambique. Kevin Pitzer proved an absolute jewel with his freely-given assistance in moments of crisis and many, many others were on hand when I needed them.

And then of course, there is my daughter Deborah. In my self-centred desire to walk the length of the Zambezi, I didn't think about the effect on her. Now I know and I can only grovel at putting her through what I did and yet she was still there for me whenever I needed help.

What a wonderful lass she is!

After the walk was over, so many people helped put my somewhat scrambled senses back together again. Susan and John Hammill in Johannesburg, Sue and Marque Dalais in Durban and Barry and Marina Woan in Margate were particularly lavish with their hospitality and it was hugely appreciated.

I have mentioned most of the folk who helped along the way in the text, but to anyone I have inadvertently left out, please know that without you, I could not have succeeded in my venture and I am profoundly grateful.

Writing a book is often an adventure in itself and this one has proved more difficult than most. Doctors Bridget Jorro and Begonia Bovill, together with Shelagh Brown put me back on track when the 'bugs' were getting me down, Jilly Wright was once again an absolute star with the manuscript and my daughter in law, Gillian Lemon deserves special mention for sorting out my photographs and designing another splendid cover.

As for the two men to whom this book is dedicated, words seem somehow inadequate to sum up all that they did for me, not only in their assistance on the ground, but also in the lift they gave to a very battered spirit.

My sincere thanks to you all.

David Lemon

Other books by David Lemon

Ivory Madness: The College Press 1983

Africa's Inland Sea: Modus Press 1987

Kariba Adventure: The College Press 1988

Rhino: Puffin Books 1989

Man Eater: Viking Books 1990

Hobo Rows Kariba: African Publishing Group 1997

Killer Cat: The College Press 1998

Never Quite a Soldier: Albida Books 2000

Never Quite a Soldier: Galago Books 2006 **(South African edition)**

Blood Sweat and Lions: Grosvenor House Publishing 2008

Two Wheels and a Tokoloshe: Grosvenor House Publishing 2008

Hobo: Grosvenor House Publishing 2009

Soldier No More: Grosvenor House Publishing 2011

Cowbells Down the Zambezi: Grosvenor House Publishing 2013

The Poacher: Socciones Editoria Digitale 2016

A Few Readers' comments on Cowbells Down the Zambezi

I was gripped from the start; a book full of emotion and an inspirational read about an epic journey of a determined and brave man who found strength and courage against the odds. Claire Prosser.

David Lemon shares a revealing and compassionate insight into the people he meets who live along the banks of the Zambezi. Is he mad, courageous or an adventurer to rate with the best? You must read this book to make up your own mind. A. Fleming

A great read - heart stopping, heart-warming and humbling. J.J. Wright

A revealing and intriguing book. We look forward to the next one. L. Higginson

Cowbells brings back many wonderful memories. Knowing the terrain and temperatures that David Lemon experienced it is a wonder that the 'Old Boy' lived to tell the tale. The hospitality of the lakeshore rural African was always a part of their makeup and they would have been offended if he refused to partake. Maxwell.

What a fantastic book. A gripping account of walking the Zambezi. An amazing journey for anyone, let alone a 68yr old man carrying a huge weight on his back. Can't wait for the next book. S. Young.

The latest - and greatest - from David Lemon. I've been waiting to read this book - and it was so worthwhile!! G.

And the other view

A grumpy old man moans and groans on a "walk" down the Zambezi, sponging off Zambezi riverfolk who can ill-afford to give up their time and food. Poorly written too. Mutare.

Not much I can say to that last one I'm afraid.

FOREWORD

I first met David Lemon in Johannesburg when he was recovering from cerebral malaria.

Our next meeting was a few weeks later at Nyakatiwa in Mozambique. At the time, he looked exhausted, tired and very thin, but that was only on the outside. The sparkle in his eyes told us a different story. He was slightly smiling the entire time. It was so obvious that this man standing right in front of myself and the ZDF crew was absolutely at peace with himself. He looked like someone who was just about to accomplish a big dream in his life, someone who was just about to achieve something almost impossible, as indeed he was.

We had heard about his problems and the setbacks, including the malaria but here he was, still very much in charge of the situation.

"Some people climb mountains," he told me quietly. "The Zambezi is my mountain."

Crossing the river to the island of Chinde that Sunday afternoon, he told me some of the things he had experienced with his two brave companions, Moffat Barnabus and Isiah Tito over the preceding four hundred kilometres. Chinde was the end of their truly amazing journey and I think the three of us in the crew felt honoured and privileged to be allowed to film these last moments of his walk for our documentary about the Zambezi.

The next day we followed him, when he was 'marching' the last few hundred metres to the actual ocean. It was low tide, so the walk was further than usual, but he didn't seem to mind the extra distance.

As we walked, he told me exactly how he felt about the magic of this beautiful river, the Mighty Zambezi.

"The river made me stronger, it gave me the self confidence that believe it or not, I always lacked. The Zambezi has given me unbelievable memories: it was just such a wonderful experience. For me the Zambezi will always be the mother of all rivers. It might not be the biggest one, but it's got an atmosphere that is totally unique. It has undoubtedly improved me as a person too."

In all my years as a correspondent, I have never been moved as I was by David's statement. He was characterising this amazing river just perfectly. I had travelled it quite a bit with my team, but it was only when I started reading this great book that I began to truly understand the Zambezi and what makes it so special.

And it was David's obvious contentment with himself in those magic moments that taught me even more and I will remember this for the rest of my life. Never stop dreaming your dreams and never stop trying to fulfill those dreams, no matter how old you are.

A few metres before his bare feet touched the sea, David dropped his hiking stick and quickened his pace. He was clearly very moved, but 'Here we go fellas' was all he said.

What a man and what an inspiring book he has written. Thank you, David for allowing me to share that wonderful experience.

Timm Kroeger,

Bureau Chief and Correspondent,

Johannesburg Bureau

ZDF German Television,

South Africa.

PROLOGUE
(Back on the Road)

I woke before the dawn, my blanket soaked with overnight dew. Curling myself into a ball, I blew warm air into my palms, but cold from the ground ate into my bones and my aching muscles seemed to groan with the pain.

I groaned too, but stayed as motionless as possible until the dawn chorus of the bush was in full cry.

The ground hornbills – those ungainly-looking 'turkey buzzards' of Africa were the first awake and their booming calls sounded like the tympani of mighty drums. I smiled in the knowledge that I was back on the road and once again in my favourite surroundings.

'Gerrupwillyou' a grumpy francolin shrieked at his mate and she replied with similar cackling irritability. Guinea fowl chinkled as they embarked on another day of foraging and from the river, a fish eagle shrieked his awe inspiring challenge to the new day. Smaller birds joined in the chorus, the emerald-spotted wood dove's hauntingly repetitive call making me smile. Whenever I heard the emerald spotted – or green spotted as the 'experts' have now renamed him – I know I am back in the bush.

I was home again and loving it, but it was time to face the day myself. Easing out of the bedroll, I crawled across to the ashes of my fire. They looked white and dead, but Mopani wood burns for days and I carefully arranged a few dry twigs and then blew on the ashes below them. White powder flew into my face and I cursed myself. Why do I always make the same mistake? A little more circumspectly I blew again and after a few gentle breaths, the fire made a little whoomping noise and burst into life. Larger twigs were placed carefully over the originals and within a couple of minutes I had a good blaze going.

My billy still contained tea from the previous evening and that was far too precious to waste. The billy was soon on the flames, while I took containers down to the river for more water. Daylight was seeping through the trees and the bush sounds were everywhere. Inland, a lone hyena whooped an eerie farewell to the night and impala rams grunted and roared at each other in the joys of the rut.

They would spend their day arguing and fighting until the best of them had established his dominance and would become lord and master to the ladies of the herd. The vanquished males would stay just out of his reach and watch for him to make a mistake, so that they could indulge in a little kidnapping and have a few ladies for themselves. It was all part of my bushveld world – a world I had abandoned in painful despair only fifteen months previously.

Now I was back in wild Africa and although I knew that the next few months would be filled with a great deal of pain and hardship, it felt good to be on the road again.

Emerging from the trees in which I had camped, I interrupted a kudu bull on the opposite bank. He was having his morning drink and at my appearance, his head jerked up and he gazed at me across fifty metres of gently flowing water. I stood still and for a long moment, looked into his large limpid eyes, mentally assuring him that I posed no threat to his safety.

The bull was unconvinced and with a sudden bound, he was away up the bank, powerful haunches propelling him forward like the world class athlete that he was. With huge spiral horns laid back across his withers, the bull disappeared into the trees and I mentally apologised to him for disturbing his ablutions.

After studying the water for crocodiles, I dipped my mug in and carefully filled my water bags. They were made of reinforced plastic and 'guaranteed' to be shockproof, but water is heavy and I would only carry half a litre with me when I walked on. That meant staying close to the river, but that was the point of my expedition in any case.

Wandering back to my very basic little camp, I sniffed appreciatively at the smoke from the fire. Mopani wood is very hard and when it burns, gives off a wonderful aroma that seems to linger in the trees.

My tea was boiling, so I filled my mug, pulled up a log to sit on and reflected on the moment and the day ahead. What would it bring I wondered? When I had started my walk at the river source two years previously, I had been confident that I could deal with any particular problems that the Mighty Zambezi would throw at me. Gazing down at the tiny spring that becomes one of the greatest rivers in the world, I felt full of enthusiasm for the task ahead. At sixty-seven I was pretty old to be embarking on a solo walk across wildly undeveloped countryside, but I was sure that I would cope and achieve my ambition of becoming the first man in recorded history to walk the entire length of the fourth longest river in Africa.

At my advanced age I was doubtless being foolishly optimistic and one hundred and eighty-seven days later, I had been forced to abandon my attempt. I was a physical wreck and no longer had the strength to put one foot in front of the other or to cope with my enormously heavy pack. My teeth were falling out through malnutrition, my skin was covered in livid bruises, I had lost thirty-four kilograms in weight and my mind was completely addled. I cried a lot and sometimes laughed hysterically at I knew not what. Half the time, I didn't know where I was or why I was there. I fell repeatedly and was lucky not to suffer serious injury on occasion. Local people had gone out of their way to help me and to them I will always be grateful, but when I reached the little Zambian town of Siavonga beside the Kariba dam wall, I gave up. I had had enough and by degrees, I wandered back to England, wrote my book **Cowbells Down the Zambezi**, regained most of my lost weight and prepared myself to go back and start again from where I had left off.

Two years after my cheerfully naive beginning, I was wiser and considerably humbler. The Zambezi had proved itself a formidable adversary and there had been a number of occasions during my first six months of walking when I was sure that I would die. Food had sometimes been scarce, so that weight dropped off me at an alarming rate, malaria had added to my problems and the terrain through which I travelled had sapped my energy and my confidence.

I had been given a hero's welcome at Siavonga and local folk, both black and white had provided an incredible amount of support. Nobody mentioned the fact that I had failed in my endeavour, but that failure ate like sour acid into my heart. I wasn't accustomed to being beaten and for a very long time I felt a huge sense of self-disgust. I had let everybody down and they had all been too polite to tell me so. To be honest, I didn't like myself very much at the time. Failure is a bitter pill indeed to take.

After fourteen long months when my thoughts, dreams and plans centred on the Mighty Zambezi, I had returned to Siavonga, reasonably fit again and having regained most of my lost weight. Local people were pleased to see me back and there was a big send off when I restarted my walk. Two of my grandchildren had come out from England and my old friend Audrey McGeorge had driven up from Cape Town to join me for the first two days of walking. A Rastafarian from Lusaka had also joined our little party and he proved to be a real tonic. Alexis Phiri is a wild life sculptor whose life size works are displayed in a number of Zambian cities. The amazing part of it is that his statues and figurines are made out of ordinary discarded rubbish, yet they appear incredibly life like. He was wonderful company too and was to play a further part in my journey although I didn't know that when I shook his hand before hitting the trail once more.

It had been an excellent start to the second leg of my journey. For thirty-six kilometres we walked and camped as a party before I left them at a riverside camp and went on alone. My granddaughter Zara Taylor had led the way and amazed me with her stamina. She had been very ill for months and I hadn't really wanted her along, but she proved me wrong with her usual winning smile.

Half way through the first morning I was walking with Alexis when he suddenly blurted out that his father was being buried at eleven o'clock that day.

"Why on earth are you here then?" I demanded with some horror. "Surely you should be with your family?"

He laughed although his eyes were sad.

"My Dad is dead and I know he would rather I was making history with David Lemon and his walk than sitting around with other mourners at his funeral."

To say that I was touched would be an understatement. I know how much family funerals matter in African culture and although it was supremely flattering, Alex' wonderful gesture disturbed me for a while. At eleven o'clock I ensured that we all stopped by the side of the road and bowed our heads in prayer for the Rasta's departed parent. It was the least I could do, but from that moment on, Alex the Rasta and I became firm friends.

It was all great fun and we laughed a lot over two days of walking together, but deep down inside I was a worried man. I knew what lay ahead and knew how it would tax my strength and my resolve. There would be pain: there would be worry and there would be times of deep despair. With one thousand eight hundred and thirty-nine kilometres behind me, I only had a thousand or so to go, but I quailed inside when I thought about them.

Nevertheless, I was committed so there was no chance of backing out. My sponsors, Cowbell of Ndola (they manufacture powdered milk) had poured a great deal of money into the venture and others had given me so much in the way of loving support that I could not let them down.

Besides, I knew that I would not be able to live with myself if my little adventure remained incomplete. I had to reach the Indian Ocean or I would spend the rest of my life regretting it.

All these thoughts and more rattled around in my mind as I drank sweet, smoky tea beside my fire. I was deep in the Lower Zambezi now so had made excellent progress. My body still ached abominably and I hated my heavy pack with rare passion, but I knew that the pain would ease as I became fitter and stronger, so felt that I could cope. Ahead of me was the National Park, where I would be escorted by a game scout and beyond that was Mozambique and an entirely new set of challenges. It was a question of pushing myself through the next three weeks or so and once I reached the border, I would be that much closer to the sea and the end of my adventure.

Across the river in Zimbabwe, I heard elephants shriek to each other and it was a sound to soothe my troubled spirit. Whatever happened, I was back in the surroundings that I loved and as I prepared to face the day ahead, I had a sudden feeling of confidence that I would make it.

With a smile in my heart, I gathered up my bedding, washed out my mug and doused the fire. Lifting the pack on to my back was still an enormous strain – it weighed well over thirty kilograms – and I uttered an audible grunt as it settled into place, but after a last look around to ensure I had left nothing behind. I moved onto the tiny path I had been following the previous evening and headed East.

I was well and truly back on the road.

PART ONE
(Walking into Trouble.)

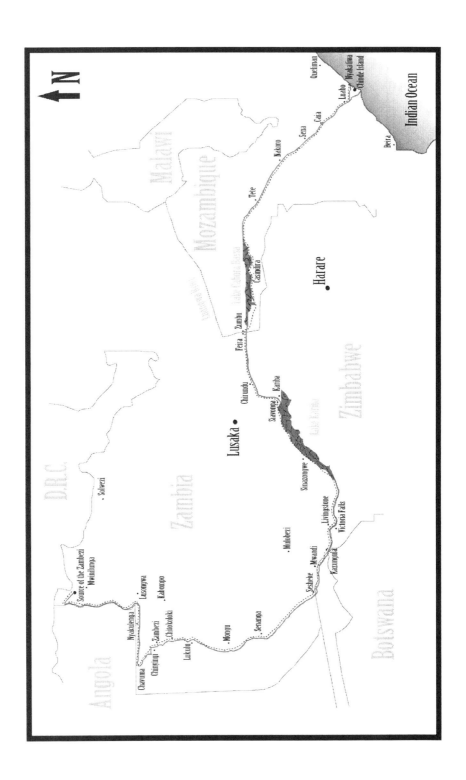

CHAPTER ONE
(Memories at Chiawa)

"I will get you some food. You must be very hungry."

I wasn't but the offer was so genuine that I accompanied Jacob Katiyo right across Chiawa Village, a sprawling collection of mud huts and small brick buildings nestling on the banks of the Zambezi

As we walked, Jacob proudly told me that he was a qualified Safari Guide and pointed out various trees to prove it.

"That one is the mighty baobab," He sounded as though he was quoting from a book as he gestured toward the bulbous forest giant. "It's proper name is *adansonia digitata*. Did you know that?"

I did but it would have been a shame to spoil his moment, so I contented myself with an admiring look. Jacob went on to point out the trail of a snake in the hot dust and I grunted my agreement with his diagnosis.

"That was a python going through the village last night."

As we made our way between the houses, Jacob darted a suddenly anxious look at me.

"You do eat Zambian food I hope? We only have nshima and fish relish."

Nshima or sadza as it is known in Zimbabwe is a porridge made from ground maize that is boiled and stirred into a glutinous paste. It is pretty tasteless but forms the staple diet of people throughout Central and Southern Africa. I assured Jacob that I enjoyed the stuff and smiled inside as I remembered some of the food I had eaten during the first part of my walk. There had been the night I spent near Lukulu with Brian Matondo and his little family. Brian worked on a pig farm and I had visions of roast pork or chops, but when his little wife Pauline approached with our supper, he had shown the same anxiety that Jacob had just displayed.

"You do eat rat, don't you?" Brian asked a little hesitantly and although I had never actually sat down to such a meal before, I told him that of course I did. Rat it was too. When the covers came off the plates, there were two recognisable rodents, roasted and lying on

3

their backs with their legs in the air. I had eaten roasted field mice in the past, but this was different. Stifling my uncertainty, I chipped a piece off mine and chewed delicately, willing myself to show no expression. Rolling a handful of nshima into a ball, I attached another small piece of rat to it and chewed with slightly less enthusiasm than normal.

It was delicious and I soon finished off my meal and complimented my host on how good it had been. I would heartily recommend roast rat to anyone who has a mind to try it.

On other occasions I had eaten boiled vervet monkey, hippopotamus, guinea fowl, Mopani worms and a few unidentifiable substances that I didn't really care to think about. I had caught and roasted flying ants myself and on a few occasions, even managed to catch a few bream with the collapsible rod I carried with me. None of these foods had done me any harm and I reckoned I could cope with whatever Jacob's womenfolk dished up for us.

In the event, it was dried fish boiled in water and although this has a slightly acrid taste, I had eaten a great deal of the stuff during my months on the road and almost come to enjoy it. As we ate, I questioned Jacob as to where he had received his training.

"I am a graduate of Conservation Lower Zambezi," He told me proudly and my interest deepened. I had exchanged a number of emails with Ian Stevenson of CLZ and he had invited me to 'drop in and see the work we are doing with local people.'

If Jacob was a typical example of that work, I was already impressed and as we sat under a thatched shelter with our food, my interest in Mr Stevenson's organisation deepened. An open-backed truck thundered by on the road beside the village and it was filled with camouflage-clad, rifle-wielding men and women, obviously on their way to somewhere.

"That is a patrol on their way to CLZ from where they will search an area outside the park," Jacob nodded knowledgably. "They will be on the lookout for snares and pit traps. They will also try and capture any poachers they may come across. It is dangerous work because many of the poachers are armed with assault rifles these days."

The truck had halted in the road and we were approached by a grizzled veteran in camouflage uniform. He wore the shoulder tabs of a colonel, but greeted Jacob with obvious warmth. I was introduced as 'My friend David who is walking to Mozambique.'

The colonel studied me with hooded eyes and I wasn't sure he approved of what he was seeing. I didn't really blame him. A thin, unshaven, white geriatric wearing a torn shirt – I had caught it in a thorn bush – was not the sort of figure to inspire confidence in that part of rural Zambia.

I explained what I was doing and added that I hoped to see Mr Stevenson at CLZ.

"We can take you," He offered but the thought of sharing the back of a truck with at least sixteen people did not appeal, so I gently turned him down. We chatted a while and then he and his crew drove off on their anti-poaching mission.

I asked Jacob if there was a specific route I should take to reach the conservation camp and he laughed.

"It is easy to find," He assured me. "Just follow this road until it turns left into some mountains. Then it bends back to the river and there you will find the camp."

It seemed a convoluted way of getting where I wanted to be and I wondered whether it would be easier to merely follow the river. After thinking on it for a moment, Jacob shook his head.

"The bush along the river is too thick," He said firmly. "There are places that you will never get through."

"And how far is it to the CLZ camp if I go by road?" I asked a little plaintively. I really didn't want to move inland.

Jacob's brow furrowed in thought and he scratched at the side of his nose.

"*Bechana kachana*," He said and I smiled. We had been talking in a mixture of English and the vernacular with a little bit of the local patois, Chilapalapa thrown in. The two words came from the latter and literally translated, they mean 'a little bit very far.'

When I put this to my companion, he enthusiastically nodded his head.

"That is right," He told me. "If you walk, it will be a little bit very

5

far. You should have gone with the truck."

But my walk down the Zambezi was not about travelling in trucks and I decided to prove Jacob wrong and stick as closely as possible to the Zambezi. A little bit very far it might be, but with over two thousand kilometres already behind me, I didn't think it would take me more than three or four days, even battling my way through rough countryside. It was nearly four weeks since I had left Siavonga and I had trimmed down and was well on the way to being very fit once more. After Conservation Lower Zambezi, I would be in the National Park and after that, it was but a short step to Mozambique. Although nobody seemed quite certain as to the actual length of the river, I reckoned that I would have a maximum of eight hundred kilometres to go when I reached the Mozambique border.

Mind you, the prospect of reaching that country provided me with more worries. Most Zambians spoke excellent English, but in Mozambique, I would have to rely on my very basic knowledge of Portuguese and that added to my anxieties. I had been turned back when attempting to enter Angola and as a result had wasted weeks arguing with Portuguese speaking officialdom. Would I have the same problems again? I didn't know but the prospect was a daunting one.

That evening in Chiawa, I lay on the ground, gazing up at the night sky of Africa – so bright, so magnificent and so utterly mesmeric. Jacob had set his own bedding up a few metres away and chattered into the darkness. Music from the local 'tarven' drifted through the village, but it was muted by distance and didn't really worry me.

"Tell me about your walk so far, Sekuru," Jacob asked quietly. "You must have met many Zambians along the way."

That I certainly had. As a Zimbabwean, I had been a little wary about wandering through what had once been 'enemy territory,' but I had spent much of my early life in what was then Northern Rhodesia, so felt a certain affinity for the country, which was not misplaced. Besides, my sponsors, Cowbell of Ndola were based in Zambia and sticking to the Northern bank of the river meant that I did not need to endure the border formalities of Namibia, Botswana or Zimbabwe. So it was that I relied on the people of Zambia and how well, they had looked after me.

That many of them considered me mad was never in doubt.

"Surely you are too old," was put to me on many occasions and others asked whether I thought I was David Livingstone. Yet for all their doubts, they did everything possible to assist me and few of them would accept my offered payments or if they did, they would apologise for their temerity. But these were terribly poor people and I was always happy to part with cash or fish hooks to show my gratitude for services rendered.

Without the River Folk of rural Zambia, I would almost certainly have died along the way and I tried to tell Jacob about some of them. The vast panoply of African stars above us helped with my narrative and I murmured quietly to my companion well into the early hours.

* * *

There could be no doubt that during my one hundred and eighty-seven days 'on the road.' I had mixed with all sectors of Zambian Society.

In fact, it had started even before I left the place where the Zambezi began, some fifty kilometres north west of Mwinilunga. A couple of days before leaving for the source, I held a press conference in Lusaka with Given Lubinda, then the Minister for Tourism and Foreign Affairs. How he combined two such important portfolios, I couldn't imagine, but he was a short, chunky man, powerful in both physique and personality.

The Minister told me that I was 'a very brave man,' but as he had recently done a bungee jump off the Victoria Falls bridge, that was a compliment easily deflected.

"I could never do that," I assured Mr Lubinda and he countered by saying that it was part of his job and only took a second or two, whereas my proposed adventure would take many months. He had a point I suppose, but I still would not put a piece of elastic around my ankle and jump into space.

Apart from that little difference of opinion, we had an amicable exchange of views and he gave me a letter of support that helped me immensely over succeeding weeks and months.

"You met Mr Given," Jacob sounded impressed through the darkness. "That is a very good man and he doesn't lie like most politicians."

With that I could only agree.

Another hugely important and influential Zambian I had met had been Chief Inyambo Yeta, the senior chief of the Lozi people. I wanted to talk with him about the Peace Park Foundation's plans to create a number of trans border parks in Zambia, but it hadn't proved easy. Just getting into his presence necessitated being interviewed by a panel of his senior Ndunas in a tribal Court room and they questioned me minutely on my intentions. I had not enjoyed the grilling, but it proved worth it in the end.

The chief was a colourful character and we shared many views on wild life conservation, so although I had only been allowed ten minutes of his time, this went on to very nearly an hour. It was a friendly interview and even though I had been briefed on how to bow and clap when the Great Man spoke, I forgot all that and we chattered away like two old friends. When we parted, Chief Inyambo Yeta gave me a big hug and my personal escort, Nduna Lubinda nearly turned pale with horror at this breach of protocol.

But apart from the Minister and the Lozi chieftain, there had been so many others who had made an impression on me. Some of them were wealthy or influential, others just rural tribesmen desperately trying to eke out a living, but without exception they had wanted to help. Many of them had difficulty feeding their families, but despite my protests, would insist on finding food for the wandering geriatric and waving away my offers to pay for it.

"That is the custom," Jacob murmured and it was, but that didn't make it any less amazing and humbling for me.

Wherever I went through rural Zambia, children would follow in my footsteps and when I sat down for a chat with local people, the same children gathered in respectful lines, just to gaze at my face and listen to my voice.

"They have never seen a white person before," A village elder called John Chipoya told me. "They think you must have come from another world."

I suppose I had but it was sobering to think that I was the first white person these children had seen. This was the multi-cultural, computerised age of the twenty-first century, but here in rural Zambia, people still inhabited the world they had lived in for centuries. The children knew nothing about computers, iPads, televisions, power tools or electric lighting. I photographed many of them and their astonishment at seeing themselves on the little screen of my camera was always comical to behold. Cell phones were sometimes seen in the hands of young men, but these were used to blast music out at all times of the day and night rather than for what they were designed. Nobody read books and they made their own entertainment without electronic toys or video games. None of them had tasted tea or coffee while ice cream and chocolate were unheard of.

Yet they seemed sublimely happy and wherever I went, I saw radiant smiles and heard the sounds of whistling or singing. Women waved shyly at my passing, while men went out of their way to find out who I was and where I was going. Children followed me for as long as they could, with their eyes wide while they exchanged whispered comments on this strange creature in their midst.

It all seemed so very innocent and heart-warming. I often feel that the frenetic inanity of life in the western world has a great deal to answer for.

"Did you pray to God to keep you safe?" Jacob asked and I pondered the question. Educated by Jesuits, I gave up on religion as soon as I could, but in the simple surroundings of the African bush, the presence of a Deity was always to be felt.

Besides, Zambia is a deeply Christian country and there were rudimentary churches in every village. At Tachitemba, there had been five such edifices and when I asked my guide at the time why they didn't amalgamate and pray together, he appeared horrified.

"But they all have different religions," Merius told me. "That one is Catholic, that one Seventh Day and that one Jehovah's. I suppose they must have different Gods so how can they pray together?"

I didn't think he quite had the point, but if the villagers were happy, who was I to interfere.

In Western Zambia, I had called into two very different missions, set on either side of Zambezi Town. Having come across a modern looking suspension bridge across the river, I asked locals about it and was directed to Chinyinge Mission where a Catholic priest, Father Paul kindly allowed me a small bedroom and abundant water to wash both myself and my clothes. Having allocated myself a day off, I explored the mission and was impressed.

Chinyinge was a sprawling collection of small but modern houses with a store, a clinic, a school and an imposing church. This was placed beside a traditional African village and the two establishments seemed to seamlessly merge into each other. I wandered around and everyone I encountered seemed cheerful and friendly. Father Paul and his priests fed me well and I spent a restful day on the seminary veranda reading and enjoying the peaceful bustle of the place.

That evening I attended Mass in the church and although the service was conducted in the local Lunda language, Father Paul gave his sermon in English. In it he referred to me and invited everyone in his substantial congregation to pray for 'this very brave man.'

Brown eyes swivelled towards me and I squirmed, but they were all friendly and the prayers offered by those lovely people were obviously effective as I am still here to write this book.

I left Chinyinge and its incredible bridge the following day and as I wandered down a tiny track beside the river, I felt curiously uplifted by my twenty-four hours with genuinely good people. I have always felt a certain antipathy toward missionaries, but Father Paul and his colleagues were obviously doing a great deal of good for the people of the area.

Four or five days later, I wandered into Chitokoloki Mission, a different sort of establishment, run by a Canadian missionary called Gordon Hanna. Gordon had been there for thirty years and greeted me warmly. He took me home where his wife Ruth tutted over the state of my clothing. Walking in the bush is not conducive to neatness or cleanliness, but I was soon showered, shaved and the offending garments whisked away to be sorted out. A delicious meal followed and I found myself fascinated by the lovely couple who had given up their lives to look after tribespeople in one of the most remote corners of the world.

Chitokoloki means 'Silver Water' in the Lozi language and when I sat on Gordon's veranda that evening I could see how the name came about. The Zambezi flowed across my line of vision and looked like a vast band of burnished metal across the Zambian plains. It was breathtakingly beautiful and I couldn't help feeling that it was no wonder that everyone I met in this enchanted spot wore a smile as big as Africa itself.

When I asked Gordon what brand of Christianity he espoused, he firmly shook his head.

"We are just Christians," He said simply. "We have no particular religious bent and no ecclesiastical hierarchy such as bishops and priests to use up our funds."

It seemed that Chitokoloki is supported by benefactors all over the world and the hospital there is the best equipped in Zambia.

"When we need something we all pray for it," Gordon smiled. "I know it sounds far-fetched, but we were desperate for an aeroplane to ferry patients around. A couple of years ago, two visiting Americans suddenly offered us an aircraft without being asked and when I chose a particular model, it was duly delivered. Shortly afterward I received a letter from a young man in Lusaka informing me that he was an experienced pilot and would love to fly our plane for us. We built the airstrip ourselves and were even given a heavy roller with which to flatten the runway."

Other much-needed items such as vehicles, boats and a five-ton truck had also been donated and Gordon was obviously very proud of the little empire he ran with the power of prayer.

I left Chitokoloki feeling that perhaps my ready cynicism in matters ecclesiastical was taking a battering. Folk like Gordon and Ruth, Father Paul and a few more I was yet to meet impressed me with their simple piety and the way they spend their lives helping and caring for the tribal folk around them.

This modern world needs more people like them.

Mind you, I occasionally wondered about the Christian ideals they were imparting to the local people. Outside the little town of Zambezi, a brick maker put his hands on my shoulders, looked deep into my eyes and told me that he knew exactly who I was.

"You are Jesus Christ," He told me solemnly. "You have come back to walk through the wilderness again."

It was a little flattering I suppose, but to balance it out, children in Sinazongwe ran sway screaming at my approach.

"The kids think you are a Satanist," A friendly lass called Mavis told me. "They are said to be taking children for their body parts in this area."

To go from Jesus Christ to Satanist in the eyes of village people was a little confusing, but I coped.

* * *

"What about women?" Jacob asked drowsily. "Did you meet many of them?"

Strange how the thoughts of young men always return to the same topic!

Women in rural Zambia tend to be shy and retiring in the company of their men folk, but whenever I encountered them on their own, they were vociferously curious and their questions tended to be far more personal than those of the men.

But the tribal system is rigidly misogynistic and in general, women would smile shyly and get on with their chores when I entered a village. An exception was Eleanor who was married to Thadeus, the deputy headman at Chuunga. She took one look at my worn appearance and took me under her wing, feeding me far more often than she fed her numerous family members and talking quietly with me while everyone else was busy or chatting under the village tree.

Due to circumstances I stayed three days at Chuunga and when I left, I gave Eleanor a tiny Maglite torch as a keepsake. The poor lass looked as though she was going to cry so I gave her a hug as well.

On another occasion I was passing a remote village above the Sioma Ngonye Falls when I was hailed from within.

"Grandfather, Grandfather where are you going?" A pretty young woman in a black tee shirt and red chitenge skirt ran out on to the track and confronted me. She beamed when I tried to explain my venture. Her name was Bridget and I defy anyone even of my advanced age to refrain from loquacity when being questioned by an admiring and very pretty young woman. When I stammered to a halt, she smiled and told me to stand still. Then she planted a big kiss on each of my cheeks and hugged me to her bosom.

"You are a great man," She told me. "But I need you to take my photograph please."

I readily agreed and she ran back into the village, emerging a short time later with two young boys.

"My sons," she explained and with the photograph duly taken I resumed my journey, marvelling anew at the kindliness and good humour of the rural Zambians. Bridget would never see her photograph, but it is on the cover of **Cowbells Down the Zambezi** and contained in the screen saver of my computer. Every so often I am reminded of a very special Sunday morning by the photograph of a smiling young woman and her two boys.

Two other women who left an indelible impression on me during my walk through Zambia were Monde Mututwa and Simamba Mambo. They both lived in Sileli Village on the outskirts of Senanga and I met them purely by accident, having arrived in the town three days early for a resupply appointment with my sponsor, Andy Taylor of Cowbell.

Walking gently along the river bank I was wondering how to occupy myself for three days and spotting a colonial style house on the top of a hill, made my way towards it. I was hoping to rest beneath a tree in the garden while I thought things out. On the way up the hill I passed a very old – and I mean VERY old – lady tottering along a path, a hoe on her shoulder and a small bucket of water in one hand. I hesitated to offer help and she scowled at me as she passed.

The house seemed deserted when I arrived, but edging my way around what must once have been a comfortable abode I saw a group of people chatting around a fire. There was only one man among them and as Zambia is a country where misogyny is the order of the day, I asked him if he would mind me resting beneath the trees for a few hours.

"Why don't you rest in my house?" The invitation came from a small woman in her mid-fifties, dressed in tribal attire of a Tee shirt and a chitenge wrapped around her body. "It is cool in there and you will be far more comfortable."

Which was how I came to meet Judith Monde Mututwa, a political princess in her own right and a woman who proved to be one of the most interesting characters I have encountered in a lifetime of wandering.

Monde made me most welcome and when I explained my predicament and asked where I could make a small camp, she invited me to sleep on her settee and stay till Andy arrived. It was the start of a magical three days and I came to admire my hostess more and more as time went on.

The house itself had no running water or electricity, but Monde made light of it and I was very comfortable. She fed me well, although meals were cooked on the fire outside and there was always hot water on hand should I need a bath or a shave.

Monde's father, Maxwell had been Ngambela (Prime Minister) of the Barotse Royal Establishment and held cabinet posts in successive Zambian parliaments. A fiery orator, he had been arrested for treason at the age of ninety-two and although a public outcry saw him released a month later, Monde felt that the experience was what had killed him.

"A few weeks later, he was sitting in his chair and just died," She told me sadly. "He really was an interesting man and you would have liked each other."

I asked her about the elderly lady I had seen carrying water and she laughed.

"That must have been Simamba Mambo," She explained. "Simamba is our oldest resident in the village and although she is well over a hundred, still insists on doing everything for herself. I will take you to see her while you are here."

We paid a visit that evening and I came away from my meeting with Simamba Mambo feeling privileged to have spent time with a very special person. It was a typically African interview with the lady herself sitting on the floor, Monde who was acting as interpreter on a stool and me on the only chair available. Wrinkled and bowed she might have been but Simamba had a simple dignity and her mind was perfectly clear. She told me that she was 'about one hundred and five,' although that could have been a year or two either way. She talked of the past and of the great Zambezi which had been a major part of her life. She had been born in Sileli and would die there, but she had been to Zimbabwe where her late husband had worked in Bulawayo and Hwange.

What could she remember of my country, I asked gently and she grinned, showing surprisingly good teeth.

"Nice people and lovely beer," was her verdict on my homeland.

Before we left Simamba, I told her how I had seen her that morning and hadn't known whether to offer a helping hand or not. She laughed and poked me in the chest with her finger.

"I saw you too," She chortled. "A skinny old man with a big luggage on his back. What could you have done? Besides, I can carry more than you can."

It summed her up really- an indomitable spirit inside a diminutive body. She would probably live for ever and she was undoubtedly correct – she could carry more than I could.

My three days with Monde Mututwa passed all too quickly and were fun. Wherever we went, she was treated like visiting royalty and many were the questions asked as to my place in her life. My grasp of the Lozi language was too rudimentary – all I could say was 'muswili' which meant hello - for me to follow what was said, but from the girlish giggles and shy glances at me, it was obvious that the locals had me lined up as a future husband.

Monde had been married to Gilbert Nkausu, a man who held two ministerial posts in the Chiluba government a few years previously. She had travelled the world and dined in fine surroundings yet she seemed happy to live now as a tribal woman. She cared deeply about the local people and was patron of the Maxanaedi School for Orphans, Street Kids and Vulnerable Children. We paid that establishment a visit one afternoon and I was impressed with the kindly efficiency of the staff who were inevitably battling with a huge lack of spending money.

I left Monde with a kiss and a hug on the Friday and walked on toward Senanga feeling that once again my footsteps had been guided toward a meeting that would live long in my memory. It sounds vaguely snobbish, but after weeks of only the most basic conversations, it had been lovely to discourse on a variety of topics with a highly intelligent lady.

"You should have stayed and married her," Jacob murmured sleepily. "Then you would not have had to walk."

I laughed, but sleep was calling and after thanking him for looking after me and bidding him goodnight, I slipped away into dreamland.

CHAPTER TWO
(Comfort Along the Way)

It was mid-morning a couple of days later, the sun was hot and I was resting beside a rough road that ran parallel to the river. I hadn't taken Jacob's advice to go inland, but had found what appeared to be an old road and as it seemed to be heading East, I followed it.

Puffing gently on my pipe, I listened to the sounds of Africa and felt supremely content with my lot. Not for the first time in a very long life, I felt totally free. I could do what I wanted, could go anywhere and I was definitely enjoying myself. Even the ache in my shoulders seemed to have eased.

A cloud of dust signalled the advent of a vehicle from the East. I watched with mild curiosity as a land cruiser rumbled into view. Brakes screeched when the driver spotted me and I swallowed dust as the vehicle stopped beside me. There were two white men in the cab and the driver stuck his head out of the window.

"Are you the bloke who is walking the Zambezi?" He enquired and I acknowledged that indeed I was. It seemed a fairly fatuous question as I didn't think there would be too many elderly wanderers in this remote corner of the world, but I was too content to point that out. The man in the passenger seat then leaned across.

"I am Roddy Smith," He introduced himself, "and this is Troy who works with me. I used to share lodgings with your son Graeme in Kariba. How is he doing?"

There followed a few minutes of gentle gossip and just before the two men drove on, Roddy Smith invited me to stay at his lodge, Mwambashi when I came through the national park.

"Stay a while with us," He offered. "We have every comfort and you will probably need a rest by then."

I needed a rest right then and there, but I merely smiled and promised to call in should I happen to spot the lodge. It was always nice to have a little bit of comfort in prospect, but I would have a game scout with me when we reached the Park, so I wasn't sure where he would fit in with the world of luxury tourism.

After giving me slightly more precise directions to Conservation

Lower Zambezi, Roddy Smith and his companion pulled away and shrugging my pack on to my shoulders, I continued walking. The road was straight and reasonably wide, so the going was easy but as I plodded along I thought back to the various lodges and hotels I had stayed at along the way.

It had started with the pleasant but claustrophobic Ngongo Lodge in Solwezi. That had entailed a twelve day stay, largely spent arguing with Angolian (all Zambians added the 'l') officialdom. In Mongu, the local Cowbell representative had put me into a very upmarket establishment called the Majesty Lodge, but I had been in a pretty bad way at the time and somehow managed to fall during the night and cut my head. In Senanga, Andy Taylor had hired two rooms at the Senanga Safaris Lodge which was owned by Charles Mututwa, Monde's cousin. That had been fun as Andy had brought his girlfriend Talitha along and Charles himself had entertained us with a film show on the Lozi, *Kuomboka* ceremony.

Kuomboka is the ceremonial passage of the *Litunga* (King) when the Zambezi begins its annual encroachment on the plains and the royal palace has to be moved inland to Limilunga. This movement cannot begin until the royal drum m*utango* is beaten and when the *Litunga* moves, he takes all his possessions with him on two royal barges.

"I was privileged to be an oarsman on the royal barge, *Nalikwanda* that year." Charles told us and his eyes shone with pride. "It is the greatest honour any young Lozi man can aspire to and it was an occasion I shall never forget."

When I moved on from Senanga, I couldn't help reflecting that for all their past glories, the Mututwa family has a wonderful future ahead of it with two strong characters like Charles and Monde at the helm.

My next stay in shelter of a sort – I normally slept on the ground in patches of forest – was at the Sioma Ngonye Falls. The Victoria Falls are rightly famous throughout the world and visitors flock there in their thousands, but few of those visitors realise that two hundred kilometres upstream is another waterfall that is every bit as spectacular.

The Sioma Ngonye Falls consists of five distinct waterfalls, set in a gigantic horse shoe of roaring, foaming water with towering columns of spray reaching high into the Zambian sky. The noise from the falls is terrific and I learned that the word 'ngonye' refers to the booming sound of water rushing through rocks. Officially these were the Ngonye Falls, but the nearest village was Sioma and most Zambians in the area referred to them as the Sioma Ngonye Falls.

There was a splendid little camp site close to the falls and although it was basic, there was hot water provided and it suited me down to the ground. Flip Nel who was in charge of the local visitors' centre lived in the camp site, although his domain was a wooden house rather than the thatched shelter with which I was provided. Flip was a year younger than me and had been a ranger in the Kruger National Park for thirty years. He invited me to share his supper and we sat up late into the night, talking quietly and setting the world to rights.

At one stage I commented that we were a typical pair of old codgers, sitting with our pipes by the fire and telling stories of the days when elephants roamed the land. He smiled gently.

"That is true enough. We weren't born when the continent was being opened up, but we have seen much that will never be seen again."

It was a sobering thought and I drifted off to sleep that night feeling privileged, not only to have seen this magnificent part of Africa but also to have spent time with a man who loved the wild places as much as I did.

It is always nice to know that one is not alone in one's eccentricities.

* * *

My visit to Mutemwa Lodge began badly. That morning I was lost, had cut myself badly and was covered in mud after a couple of bad falls. I didn't feel I could go on and inwardly debated using my sponsored satellite phone and getting Andy Taylor to send someone to pick me up.

It was probably the lowest point of my walk at that stage and while I was trying to motivate myself, I heard a heavy engine start up not terribly far away. It rumbled into the morning and I knew that where there was a motor, there had to be people. As I wasn't even sure where the river was, I made toward the sound.

Bleeding badly and using my walking pole as a makeshift crutch, I hobbled toward the noise of the engine and suddenly found myself in an area of huge trees and gently mown green grass. A swimming pool twinkled in the sunshine and a thatched building could be seen ahead.

This was Mutemwa Safari Camp and when I asked a little fellow who appeared to be in charge whether I could wash myself and rest for a couple of hours, he told me that he would 'fetch the Madam.'

Said 'Madam' turned out to be a petite and pretty lady with a smile that must have conquered many a male heart. Behind her were three younger versions and all four of them glanced somewhat warily at this unexpected and unprepossessing visitor.

Thus I came to meet Penny Johnson and her daughters Shan, Kayla and Tammy. If it is possible for an old man to fall in love with four ladies simultaneously, I did and although I didn't realise it when I introduced myself, I was about to embark on three days of bliss that would have been unimaginable two hours previously.

Later in the day I met Penny's husband, Gavin. A rugby world cup winner with the Springboks in nineteen ninety-five, he was quietly welcoming and when we sat down to supper, almost brought me to tears. The Johnsons were devout Pentecostals and before each meal would gather in a circle, hold hands and pray for whatever they felt like at the time. It was a simple little ceremony and when Gavin thanked God for bringing me into their midst, I felt emotion welling up in my throat. For the first time in weeks, I was part of a family and before I went to bed, three of the four ladies gave me a hug and a kiss to see me through the night. Little Tammy was too shy and possibly worried by my gaunt appearance, but the following morning she greeted me with a huge smile and a hug that was very precious. It seemed I had arrived in one little girl's affections and I felt ten feet tall.

My stay with the Johnsons was truly magical and provided me with memories for life. They fed me, cosseted me and above all, surrounded me with genuine love. After dinner on the night before I left, the girls presented me with a farewell gift, consisting of a woollen 'beanie' to keep me warm through the freezing nights, a poem from Shan and a vegetable ivory key ring that I attached to my pack. I found it difficult to thank them through my appreciative tears.

Yet my visit to this idyllic spot might never have been. The engine noise that had brought me to Mutemwa came from a water pump that was run for two hours every day. When I spoke about it to Penny, she frowned.

"God is definitely looking after you," She said seriously. "We normally run the pump at four in the afternoon, so quite why it was on in the morning, I don't know. I am glad it was though."

So was I and even now, I shake my head in perplexity when I think about it. I am often asked whether I feel God about me in the bush and there is no question that on many occasions there seems to be something guiding me along. There have been so many times when I have survived only through what seemed divine intervention that it has gone way past mere coincidence. The beauty and regal grandeur of the African bush also seems to indicate a Creator with wonderful aesthetic tastes and I am always happy to accept His – 'Hers' perhaps – assistance when I am in trouble.

Maybe my meeting with the lovely Johnson family was divinely organised but I am profoundly grateful to whoever switched on that water pump.

I stayed in other beautiful places and with other nice people during my hundred and eighty-seven days on the road. There were David and Jean Moir who lived on the river bank in a palatial home outside Sesheke, Hilda Chipman Dunn who was building a beautiful lodge at Kashavati and of course, Karien Kermer who - determined to see me put on weight - fed me up for a few days in Livingstone. There were the lovely Jordaans of Siansowa who put me up for nearly a week at their Kariba Bush Camp and refused to accept payment. Sandy and Patrick Dankwertz gave me a champagne breakfast and allowed me to use their holiday cottage in Sinazongwe, while Anne-Marie and David Mynhardt gave me the use of a chalet in their gorgeous camp on the shores of Lake Kariba.

Peta and Billy Mulder entertained me right royally at their Blue Waters camp and before leaving them, I urged Peta to write a book about her life. What a time she has had! During her years of being married to Billy, she has lived in a tent, looked after lions and a variety of dangerous animals and truly led a life that would make for fascinating reading. I was sad to leave them, not so much for the comfort and friendship they had afforded me but for the stories they left untold.

In Siavonga town, my self-disgust at pulling out of the walk even temporarily was ameliorated by the kindness and concern of everyone at Eagles Rest. Steve and Carol Thompson were wonderfully kind and as with the other good folk I have mentioned, provided me with shelter, delicious food and friendship which was hugely appreciated. Yet whenever I found myself in comfortable surroundings I felt vaguely guilty that I wasn't sleeping under the stars and eating my gruel beside a Mopani fire.

Truly we human beings are complex animals.

I had stayed in two more lodges since leaving Chirundu on this leg of the trip and my sojourn at Wild Tracks with Sven and Paula Vrdoljak was particularly enjoyable. They ran nature lessons for youngsters and were a fascinating couple. Sven had been a first class rugby player in South Africa and was also a doctor of Entomology, while Paula was a former advertising executive and apparently a big wheel in African media circles.

While in their camp, I picked up a book by Kingsley Holgate and snorted when I read a passage in which he described himself as 'the Greybeard of African Adventurers.' Huh! The bloke is two years younger than I am.

Like everyone else along the way, the Vrdoljaks and their staff treated me with kindness, respect and overwhelming hospitality, so as always I had mixed feelings when it was time to move on.

Now I was approaching the Park itself and although Roddy Smith's offer was undoubtedly genuine, I knew that I would again feel guilty if I took it up.

Perhaps the heat was already addling my brain.

CHAPTER THREE
(Mwambashi and The Park)

Elephants have always been my passion in life and one of the disappointments of my first one hundred and eighty-seven days of walking was the fact that I had only seen one of the great grey giants. He panicked when he realised what I was and it was obvious that he and his immediate family had been sorely persecuted by mankind.

Sitting on a chair outside my comfortable tent at Conservation Lower Zambezi, I became aware of movement in nearby bushes. A young elephant bull appeared and wandered idly past me without turning a hair at my presence. What a wonderful moment it was and I heard more of them whickering and rumbling to each other during the night.

Ian Stevenson proved to be a cheerful soul who lived in a wooden house on the site and flew his own aircraft. He was in close contact with local representatives of the Zambian Wildlife Authority (ZAWA) and spoke to the warden at Chirundu about the game scout who was due to accompany me through the Lower Zambezi Park. Unfortunately, the warden knew nothing about it, even though Andy and I had discussed the matter – and paid out a great deal of money in fees – with a number of people in the Lusaka Headquarters of ZAWA. I had paperwork and receipts to prove it, but with Zambian bureaucracy, that meant very little.

This made me cross as quite apart from Cowbell parting with a lot of money for my benefit, part of the fee was supposed to be paid in the form of a daily allowance to the scout in question. I had no doubt – and Ian agreed with me – that the money had been diverted into someone's pocket and would never be doled out as intended.

"Africa wins again," Ian murmured and promised to arrange matters with the local warden.

Inevitably, that took time and I spent another two days at CLZ. They were interesting days though. Again I ate well and enjoyed my evenings looking out across the Mighty Zambezi. I attended a couple of briefings and debriefings with Ian's anti-poaching teams and spent some time chatting with the individuals involved. They were all young men and women who seemed to enjoy doing what they could to combat the scourge of poaching in the areas adjacent to the Lower Zambezi National Park.

I also did quite a bit of walking around local roads and tracks, enjoying the warmth, the dust and the proximity of wild life. There were few people to be seen, but elephants were plentiful and the bush was kept noisy by the rutting impala. I watched a few fights between males and admired the courage they showed – perhaps it was desperation - in taking each other on. The vanquished rams would stand in obvious sulks after a beating while the victor invariably strutted his stuff like a successful boxer after a contest.

There were other animals too and the bird life was prolific, so I really enjoyed my wait on the whims of the local warden. I was losing time, but didn't think that would matter. I could make it up later and despite all the rest periods I had enjoyed in part one of the walk, I had still averaged over nine kilometres a day.

I didn't think that was bad for a man in his late sixties.

At last Ian arrived with good news and a burly man in park-style camouflage uniform. He was introduced to me as Patrick Gondwe and I took to him at once despite the lethal looking Kalashnikov assault rifle he was wielding. That was probably just as well, as we would be walking together through what might prove difficult and dangerous terrain.

Just after six the following morning, Patrick and I wandered through the park gates to cries of encouragement from the scouts on duty. We followed a track that eventually took us back to the Zambezi and in those first few hours, we encountered elephant in number and a variety of antelope. Baboons bawled at us from treetops and a lordly bateleur eagle scowled his displeasure at our presence. It was wonderful and my heart sang at being back in wild Africa.

I had asked Patrick whether he knew where Mwambashi was and he assured me that he would take me there. I felt guilty again at taking time off, but reminded myself that I was in no particular hurry. I had no deadline for reaching Chinde, so it surely behoved me to enjoy myself as much as possible. There would undoubtedly be painful and unpleasant times ahead to counteract the good ones, so I stifled my guilt and looked forward to learning more about

Roddy Smith's friendship with my son Graeme.

With the sun high overhead and very hot, we made camp on a point jutting into the river and Patrick expressed surprise at my lack of a tent. He had a bright orange one for himself, but I explained that tents made me claustrophobic and were heavy to carry. I don't think he was convinced and he muttered something about lions. I know they are dangerous animals, but one has to be very unlucky to encounter a cat whose hunger overcomes his natural fear of humans. I have always trusted in 'Lemon's Luck' – it won me a lottery prize once – and have slept in wild places with lions around since I was a teenager.

As evening rolled down from the great escarpment across the river, a vehicle trundled along a nearby road and we waved half-heartedly. I didn't want to share my space with curious tourists, but couldn't help feeling vaguely smug when their truck suddenly sank to the axles in soft sand.

"Serves them right," I muttered uncharitably to Patrick and he smiled, but night was approaching and the three men in the vehicle dug frantically to free themselves. A winch cable was rolled out, but the only tree to which it could be attached came out by the roots and eventually Patrick and I went across to help. Branches beneath the wheels and a great deal of sweaty muscle power eventually freed the truck and two German tourists expressed their thanks. When they heard what I was doing, they were admiringly incredulous and promised to follow my progress as far as was possible in Germany.

I had already been contacted by a German television production company, based in Johannesburg. They had asked to accompany me for part of my walk, but I didn't want that. We had compromised eventually and I agreed that they could film me crossing the border or perhaps cover the finish at Chinde.

I told the German tourists that they would probably see more footage of my walk than people in England.

Patrick and I settled down soon after darkness and I slept well beneath the stars and with familiar bush sounds all around me. Hippo chortled in the river, elephants squealed and rumbled to each other and a hyena whooped from not too far away. Nightjars chattered to the stars and the booming grunts of an eagle owl seemed to resonate through the darkness.

It felt good to be home.

* * *

It had been a long, hard and very hot morning. We had covered a lot of kilometres through open Mopani country but over extremely difficult ground. It had obviously been very muddy at one stage and the mud was churned up by countless hooves and feet. Then it dried, leaving a hard crust of craters and holes that were painfully difficult to walk over. Time and again one foot or the other would turn over in a hole and I dreaded suffering a bad sprain or even a break to one of my ankles.

But the countryside was lovely, we were making excellent progress and we saw buffalo, waterbuck and impala during the morning. Patrick pointed out an elephant skull beside the dried up saucer that must have been a water hole in the rainy season and we moved across to have a look. He had seen it before and made a face as he pointed out two small holes in the front of the skull.

"Poachers," He murmured. "We found two 7,62 intermediate bullets inside the skull."

It was sad to see hard evidence of the wholesale slaughter that is going on among elephants in the wild, but we were to find further signs of wide scale poaching in the Park over the next few days.

It was around noon that my guide made an abrupt turn and led me through some thatched buildings that seemed to have unexpectedly sprung up among the trees.

"Mwambashi," He said with a smile and I felt my muscles relax with the prospect of imminent rest. A pretty lady emerged from one of the buildings and approached with a smile that warmed my heart.

"You must be David Lemon," She said. "Roddy told us you would be calling in and we have been expecting you. I am Pamela and I supervise the catering. Welcome to Mwambashi."

She held out her hand and I shook it enthusiastically before realising that my own palms were dripping with sweat and must have been awful to touch. Later on I apologised and Pam gave a tinkling laugh.

"It brought home what you must be going through with this walk of yours," She told me. "How you have survived this long in such wild country, I just cannot imagine."

Mwambashi or to give it its formal name, Mwambashi River Lodge, turned out to be a typical bush lodge, combining functional comfort with luxurious food and wild surroundings. There was a South African camera crew in residence when I arrived and their eyes were wide when Pam escorted me into the main building. They were making an advertising film promoting the camp and I watched them work with considerable fascination over the next couple of days. They were consummate professionals and even when an elephant with her calf wandered through camp one afternoon, they ignored it completely and concentrated on the piece they were filming beside the swimming pool.

Rebecca Griffiths, a pretty girl from Johannesburg introduced herself as the housekeeper and smilingly told me that the Reed Suite had been set aside for me.

A suite for me? That surely was going from the sublime to the ridiculous but I didn't argue. The thought of any proper bed was appealing.

Patrick was allocated a house in the staff quarters and before heading off for a wash and a rest, he and I sat down to an excellent lunch of quiche, cold meat and salads.

The Reed Suite was a magnificent building, constructed entirely with reeds and it was luxury indeed. I had two bedrooms to choose from, a lounge and a veranda overlooking the Zambezi together with what was surely the largest mosquito net, I had ever slept beneath. It covered two single beds set wide apart and for one, accustomed to sleeping beneath a tiny scrap of gauze each night, it seemed the size of a tennis court. I was impressed.

That evening, I met the rest of the staff and was questioned at length about the reasons for my journey and how I was doing. In return I found out quite a lot about my hosts.

Pamela Tweet was Roddy's sister and she had come up from Pietermaritzburg two years previously. A lovely lady, she had a vaguely sad aura about her and my ever fertile imagination decided that she was running from a love affair that had gone wrong. I didn't care; she prepared incredible food and although she gave credit to her staff, Roddy later told me that she had enjoyed *cordon bleu* training. It certainly showed in the meals she presented us with.

Rebecca looked very much the city executive, but told me that she had followed her boyfriend Dale Lewis to Mwambashi where he had been resident guide for nearly nine years.

"Once I saw the place, I was hooked," She smiled. "I have been here five years now and can't think of anywhere I would rather be living."

I had a wonderful couple of days at Mwambashi. They all treated me like visiting royalty and nothing was too much trouble. Although Patrick was quartered with the camp staff, we spent a lot of time together and he assured me that he too was eating like a king. Roddy and I also talked at length, mainly about the 'good old days' when he and Graeme had been young guides in Kariba and shared a house with two others. Casually I asked about one of the other two, Torben Lorgesen, who I knew had come up to Zambia a few years previously.

"I will get hold of him,' Roddy promised. "It is Sunday, so he won't be working and perhaps he can fly down"

So it was that after lunch – supremely delicious as always – Roddy and I watched as a tiny red aircraft wobbled its way in to the camp landing strip and my old friend, Torben unwound himself from the pilot's seat. Mind you, it must have been the only seat, as that little machine didn't have much space for crew members.

We spent forty minutes or so reminiscing beside that airstrip, then Torben (I had known him as a penniless youngster, but he must have been doing well) took off again, waggled his wings and disappeared towards distant Lusaka.

It is always a joy to meet up with old friends and his visit had made my day.

* * *

Three days later, we were approaching a place called Mshika where

Patrick was to leave me and be replaced by another scout. A very large bull elephant wandered past, glancing sideways at us but not showing signs of undue alarm. I stopped to watch the magnificent creature and stood transfixed with wonder, only coming back to the real world when Patrick nudged my arm and whispered urgently.

"Stand still Boss. Don't move a muscle. We have trouble."

Turning my head slowly in his direction, I saw a large male lion emerge from a clump of dense vegetation some twelve metres away and stand out in the open. It was old and its dark mane was threadbare, but it was still a formidably dangerous animal and I felt a sudden chill in my blood as I watched it. Not for nothing is the lion universally known as the King of the Beasts and although this particular specimen was hardly a prime example of majesty, it nevertheless had a presence about it that brought dryness to my throat.

Turning its head slowly, the lion gazed at Patrick and me but there was neither curiosity or interest in the look and it soon turned its head away from us. Moving with a sort of ponderous grace, the lion walked slowly away and all too soon had disappeared. Patrick looked at me and smiled.

"Shumba was too close," He said quietly. "We were lucky that he was not hungry."

"Perhaps," I agreed, although I was not convinced. Big and undoubtedly dangerous though they are, lions are seldom interested in human beings and will usually back off from any confrontation. Standing motionless as we had done took almost all risk out of the moment and I didn't think we had really been in any danger.

Sadly, that was the only lion I saw in my entire three thousand two hundred kilometre walk. It is a sad reflection of the devastating damage being caused to wild life throughout Africa. The Zambezi Valley has always been famous for its lions and there have been many instances of man eating recorded through the years, but to see only one somewhat mangy specimen in a two hundred and ninety-two day walk was truly heartbreaking.

Unlike the other lodges I had visited along the way, Mshika – I later learned that the name was to be changed to Amabezi - was truly luxurious. It belonged to wealthy Zimbabwean hunting magnate,

Charles Davey and he had obviously focussed on the richer tourists of the world. Due to a mix up in the changeover of my ZAWA escorts, I was forced to spend a night in the lodge and I found myself awestruck, but a little disturbed at the ostentatious hedonism of the entire camp. Each chalet – and there were eight – had two bathrooms, a huge bedroom, an office, lounge and veranda. The furnishings were lavishly opulent and the mosquito net was even bigger than the one that had so impressed me at Mwambashi. This one was almost as large as my house in rural Gloucestershire.

Thick rugs covered the floors and although I started counting the umbrellas contained in a specially made stand, I soon gave up. There were dozens of assorted brollies and I wondered what they were for. If it rained, two would certainly be handy for the occupants of chalet number five, but what would they do with twenty of the ruddy things?

Somehow, although it was palatially comfortable, the place just did not seem part of Africa – particularly the wild Africa in which it was located. My veranda looked out across a wide vlei area and I spent the evening watching elephant, impala, warthog and kudu wander around, but I felt sadly out of place. I suppose the place would be frequented by the very rich (Charles Davey is a Zimbabwean millionaire whose daughter Chelsy once went out with Britain's Prince Harry) but would they really feel that they were in Darkest Africa? Somehow I doubted it, but then what did I know about the other half of society?

Ian Stevenson flew in that evening to collect Patrick and take him back to Chirundu and fortunately – thanks to Ian's efforts on my behalf – I managed to link up with my new guide the following morning.

Phillip Katulula was the antithesis of Patrick though he wore the same uniform and also carried an AK47. Small and slightly built, he was a very quiet man, but he set a good pace and I was quite relieved at the lack of conversation. We were approaching the Mupata Gorge and the prospect worried me a little, but Phillip waved away my concerns. We walked hard for two long days and on the second of these, the going was terribly rough. Time and again we were forced to crawl through thickets on our stomachs and on one of these little forays, my GPS must have fallen out of its pocket. I only noticed it when we stopped for a rest beside the river and although it was a serious blow to my morale, I was not prepared to retrace my steps and search for the ruddy thing. It was basically an expensive toy and even after carrying it for months, I still didn't know how to use it properly.

Without it, I could at least revert to adventuring in my own way.

CHAPTER FOUR
(Crossing into Mozambique)

My last official resupply had been arranged to take place at the Redcliff Zambezi Lodge, but we struggled to find the place. Phillip had been great in the Park, quickly finding tracks and trails that he knew, but once outside his own environment, he seemed to lead me in every direction imaginable. We climbed hills, fought through tangled bush and occasionally found ourselves on recognisable tracks that seemed to lead nowhere.

After a long morning of hellish walking, we staggered into the lodge around midday and I met genial proprietor Hugo Erfman in his office.

"I have been expecting you," How was it that everyone seemed to know where I was, when I didn't? "Your people are due to arrive tomorrow, so you can spend the weekend with us."

'My people' were Vic and Helen Shone, dear friends from Lusaka. They duly arrived with their son Aaron and my supplies for the next six weeks and then we proceeded to enjoy ourselves. Assistant manager at Redcliff was Caroline Wezi Mfune, who was not only an expert on coffee (you don't find many of them in the Zambezi Valley) but told me that she was Malawian as well as Zambian, one parent having come from either country.

"It makes life difficult," She smiled at me. "Neither the Zambians or the Malawians really accept me as one of their own."

Tribal divides in Africa are rigidly adhered to and I understood her predicament.

But the weekend was one of pure relaxation. We sat and talked over beer, wandered around the camp and played a daft drinking game called The Box one evening with two giant South African fishermen, Marius and Shelton. On Sunday, Caroline gave Helen and I a demonstration on how to make perfect coffee, but I didn't take notes and am ashamed to say that all I can remember is the delicious taste of the beverage she prepared for us. We had boat drives up and down the river, admiring the hauntingly deep colour of the cliffs in the sunlight and Vic even caught a tiger fish. It was not a big one I'm afraid, but the successful angler posed happily with his catch for my camera and then released it gently back into the water.

The food was good and the entire weekend was a wonderful rest for me. I was close to the end of my Zambian sojourn now and rather dreading the border crossing into Mozambique. Portuguese speaking officialdom had already proved a huge problem when I attempted to cross into Angola and now I was going to face more of them. It was a sobering prospect, especially as this time I wouldn't have my friendly Mwinilunga District Commissioner, Victor Kayekesi to help me. Victor had negotiated on my behalf with the Angolan authorities and although we had lost out in the end, his efforts had been hugely appreciated.

I would have some support though, as my Rastafarian friend Alexis Phiri had promised to be meet me in Luangwa in order to see me across the border.

* * *

"Will you marry me?"

The Luangwa market place was heaving with people and for a moment, I thought I had misheard the lady, whose name she told me was Edina.

"I beg your pardon?" I queried as diplomatically as I could.

"Marry me; take me away from all this. I will make you a good wife and bear you many children."

Her first question had been as to whether I would buy some of her roasted groundnuts, so once again summoning up all the tact I was capable of, I politely declined both offers. Behind me, I heard Alex struggling to control his laughter. The burly Rastafarian had taken a bus down from Lusaka in order to see me across the border and I was glad of his company. He was staying in the District Commissioner's rest camp, which had been full when I breezed into town, but I had ensconced myself in a clean and comfortable establishment, known as the Feira Lodge. Outside the bedroom block, a giant baobab held court and the genial manager of the lodge had informed me that this was the tree beneath which slaves were

33

sold in the bad old days.

The oldest settlement in Zambia, Feira – or Luangwa as it was now known – had been a great trading centre for slavers bringing their booty down from the hinterland in order to transport the unfortunate slaves to the sea. A stone plaque beside the river told me that there were records of a fifteenth century settlement there that had been abandoned in the year 1600. In the early eighteenth century, Portuguese colonists had set up a trading centre and in 1745 a convent and church had been built by a Dominican priest, Father Pedro Das Trindade who had remained as vicar of Feira for thirty years.

The area had inevitably been subject to various minor wars and tribal altercations which had led to such a falling off of trade that the settlement was abandoned in 1830. Situated as it was at the spot where the mighty Luangwa River enters the even mightier Zambezi, it was too strategic a place to remain empty for long and in 1856, another eminent visitor was David Livingstone himself. He wrote that the town was in ruins and that he had found the broken remains of the church bell.

In 1887, John Harrison (Changa Changa) Clark, who was one of the original District Commissioners set up his administrative headquarters in Feira and maintained law and order throughout the district for many years. The Chartered Company arrived in 1902, whereupon the little settlement became an important staging post on the cattle route between Tanganyika – Tanzania nowadays - and Southern Rhodesia, which is now Zimbabwe. As the railways became more established, Feira became ever more irrelevant and now it was but little but a ramshackle village, built around the immigration post facilitating exit from Zambia and entry into Mozambique.

There were many relics of the early days around the town, including what was said to be a holding cell for slaves on the river bank, although to my jaundiced eye, this looked to be of relatively modern construction. There were also two stout poles in the shallows, which I was told had been used as mooring posts for slavers' vessels, but I couldn't help wondering how wood could have been treated in those days. Normal poles would have rotted away long before the twenty-first century dawned, so they had to have been put there as a tourist attraction. The only drawback to my cynical theory however was that few tourists ever visited Luangwa.

We were wandering around the market because Alex had decreed that he was going to make me 'a last supper' before I left Zambia and he was looking for the necessary ingredients. He muttered something to the would-be bride and she scowled at me before flouncing away.

"What did you tell her?" I asked and he grinned.

"I said that you are going across to Zumbu where you are marrying a Portuguese lady of great wealth and a fearsome temper."

"Huh!" was my only comment but I was glad he had intervened.

As with all such market places in rural Africa, there were many stalls filled with clothing and shoes that had to have been donated by various charities overseas. This was not where they were supposed to end up, but African entrepreneurs are as cunning as their counterparts elsewhere in the world and a number of people were getting very rich on the generosity of unsuspecting charity givers.

After the market, we wandered back along the dusty road into town and I stopped to photograph another baobab tree that had an almost equally large fig tree wrapped around it. As I focussed on this strange looking plant, I heard a thud and a muffled grumble from my companion. The bag in which he had been carrying his purchases had split and onions, tomatoes and assorted vegetables were rolling around in the dust. We still had a kilometre or so to go and I patted my pockets to see if I could stow any of the produce in them. As we stared somewhat helplessly at each other, a little girl who was probably five or six years old ran out from a nearby house. She was carrying an intact plastic bag, which she handed somewhat shyly to Alex.

Accompanied by the ritual curtsy, it was a charming little gesture and I commented to my companion that such kindnesses were unlikely to be encountered in the supposedly civilised western world.

Our next stop was a riverside harbour where boats of all varieties were haphazardly parked on the bank. Huge parcels of dried fish were everywhere and a local explained that they had been brought up from the great lake of Cabora Bassa and would be transported by lorry to the Democratic Republic of Congo and to Angola. It seemed that Feira was regaining some of its lost status as an important staging post for trade, but at what cost to the fish population I wondered.

Curious, I examined some of the parcels and was horrified to discover that most of the fish being removed from the lake were fingerlings or very small specimens. I had no doubt that they were tasty and probably nutritious but it seemed sad that they were being harvested so early in life and not being given the opportunity of reaching adulthood and breeding for themselves. If this unregulated slaughter continues, the lake will eventually be denuded of fish and there will be nothing to eat.

There must have been ten tons of fish stacked along that river bank and this was only one of three such harbours in Luangwa. It is the age old problem of Africa I'm afraid. Hunger is endemic so when there is food of any sort, it is eaten without any thought being given to the future.

Mind you, Alex bought some squeaker fingerlings from a vendor, so I suppose we were doing our bit toward killing off the fish as well. Squeaker are a type of catfish that possess hard, sharp barbs on either side of their head and emit a series of high pitched grunts when they are caught. They do taste nice when cooked, but I had only tasted the adult variety so wasn't sure how these would turn out.

Alex had no such worries.

"I will make you a last supper fit for any great explorer," He told me and I smiled. He was an awful flatterer, but he had my interests at heart and was to become a firm friend. On the rare occasions when I switched my cell phone on in Mozambique, there would invariably be a text message from my Rastafarian friend, saying very simply.

'Go Madala Go.'

Those little messages were to see me through some very trying times, but I didn't know that as we faced each other over a small fire and ate our 'last supper.'

It was delicious too. With the boiled squeaker, we had nshima and two relishes, one of beans and the other vegetables. It was food I wouldn't touch in normal life, but there on the banks of the Mighty Zambezi with the lights of Zumbu in Mozambique twinkling through the darkness, I ate well and congratulated my friend on his culinary skills.

Alex had promised to come over to Zumbu with me the following morning and we arranged to meet early so that I could get my exit stamp from the immigration post at the top of the hill around which Luangwa is built. Fortified by a cold beer – Feira Lodge was beside a small beer hall – I slept well that night, my dreams punctuated by Portuguese speaking squeakers being chased by a Rastafarian chef.

* * *

We had been 'reliably' informed that the immigration post opened at six, so when the allotted time arrived, we were waiting anxiously at the door. An hour later, we were still waiting and it wasn't until twenty past seven that a sleepy looking guard opened the main door from the inside and beckoned us forward. Feeling unexpectedly nervous, I handed my passport over to a very smartly uniformed young woman.

"I need an exit stamp please Ma'am," I said politely. "I am crossing into Mozambique today."

Studying the passport, the lady flicked her eyes toward my face, doubtless taking in my skeletal appearance and weary features.

"How are you travelling?" She queried and I smiled half-heartedly. Explanations as to my motives for walking the Zambezi were inclined to be tedious. I had been through it so many times before.

"On foot," I replied briefly and she tapped the passport.

"You have walked from Ndola?" Her voice rose an octave and I shook my head.

"No Ma'am, I have walked from Siavonga and before that from Mwinilunga."

Then came the inevitable, unanswerable question.

"Why?"

I could only shrug and from behind me, Alex intervened in his own language. The lady looked bored and turned back to me before my friend had finished his explanation.

"You should have left the country last week when your visa expired." She said sternly and I felt a sudden surge of panic.

"I asked for a six-week visitor's permit when I arrived," I stammered an explanation. "I thought I had another week or so."

'They only gave you thirty days. You should have checked that when the visa was issued."

She was tapping the passport in earnest now and her eyes were hard. Rather uncharitably I reflected to myself that as an elderly white man, I made an easy target for officialdom.

I was being unjust.

"I can see that you have made a genuine mistake," She snapped officiously. "But that will teach you to check your passport in future. On this occasion I will use my discretion and stamp an extra five days into your passport."

Saying which, she brought her desk stamp down hard on the offending document and I felt a wave of relief wash over me. I had been expecting a heavy fine or even a night in the local cells for my temerity in overstaying the visa. Border officials in Africa are notorious for their intransigence, but this lovely lass had used her discretion and let me go. I could have kissed her.

"Madam," I told her earnestly. "If you weren't married and I wasn't married, I would marry you today." That marriage proposal in the market was obviously still preying on my mind.

She told me that her name was Miriam and at Alex's suggestion, we trooped outside the little building for a photograph. Miriam's colleague Ingrid joined us for the picture and whenever I look at it nowadays, I cannot help a little smile.

Lemon's Luck was obviously working overtime once again and had brought me to possibly the only government official in Southern Africa who was content to 'use her discretion.'

With my triumphantly stamped passport tucked away in its

waterproof wallet and Alex clutching his 'day visa' to visit Mozambique, we made our way to the harbour. To reach Zumbu, we needed to hire a 'taxi' to get us across the wide mouth of the Luangwa River. Taxis in this context were fibreglass 'banana boats' with tiny outboard engines. Full of confidence now I approached a young man standing beside his boat.

"How much to take me across to Zumbu?" I asked and his answer knocked my new found confidence for another six.

"Fifty dollars."

Yet again I blessed my Rastafarian friend for being with me. He growled something to the boatman and that worthy visibly subsided. The asking price was reduced to five kwacha (less than a single US dollar in value) and we piled aboard, my heavy pack placed carefully in the centre of the boat. The sun was shining, the water was flat calm and I enjoyed the ride although nervousness was churning in my stomach once again. I had Portuguese speaking officialdom to face this time and I doubted whether they would be as accommodating as the lovely Miriam.

As we puttered across the water I looked back at Zambia and felt a twinge of sadness at leaving it. I had walked well over two thousand kilometres around its border, had met many wonderful people and in general had a lovely time. There had been those terrible three days spent wading across the Luena Plain and over three weeks of crawling painfully through the gorges, but in general, the going had been fairly easy and I had enjoyed myself immensely.

Now I was approaching a different country and would have to learn a great deal about local culture and practices. I would have to study my Portuguese phrase book so that I didn't make a complete fool of myself and I had to find my way around Lake Cabora Bassa and through another mighty gorge below the dam wall. It all seemed somewhat daunting but I only had about eight hundred or so kilometres to go. I sent up a brief prayer that they would be interesting kilometres and free from too much hardship.

* * *

It was late morning and hellishly hot when the banana boat taxi grounded on soft sand directly in front of Zumbu. There were other boats on the beach, many of the drivers smoking and talking together as they waited for customers returning to Zambia.

It was a colourful scene, but I was nervously sweaty and in a sudden hurry to sort out the necessary formalities. Alex barked instructions to our driver and leaving my pack in the boat, we wandered up to the immigration office, where a young man in blue uniform wearily held his hand out for my passport. I handed it over together with my letters of support from various political bigwigs as well as the Mozambique Ambassador in London. The officer's eyes widened as he read the documentation and he kept looking up at me somewhat quizzically. I wondered what he was thinking, but when he spoke, it was not what I wanted to hear.

He was pleasant enough and his English was good, but he told me that my application for entry into Mozambique 'causes problems and will have to be investigated.'

I asked why but he ignored the question and called to an overweight customs officer who was standing nearby watching proceedings. Fatty – his shirt strained to keep his belly in place – directed us back to the boat and made me open every bag in my pack and show him what I was bringing in to the country. He questioned me at length on most of the items and when I took out my Power Monkey solar battery charger, he was overjoyed and looked around for someone else to show it to. There were only the bored boatmen, but he took the little charger around them and explained in much detail how it worked. If ever the makers of this marvellous little gadget decide to open up a business in Mozambique, I can direct them towards a very keen if somewhat officious salesman.

Having reluctantly decided that I was not importing anything in the way of contraband, the fat man clapped me on the shoulder and led the way back to the immigration office and some relief from the burning sun. The immigration officer looked up at our approach and he was frowning.

"Tell me your plans again," He demanded and a little wearily, I went through the whole story. At the end of it, his frown was still in place.

"I cannot make this decision myself," I wondered what 'decision' he was wittering on about. All I wanted was an entry stamp in my passport. "We will have to go and see the chief of police."

So it was that we traipsed across to police headquarters, a battered looking building that did not have air conditioning and relied on a few geriatric fans to keep the occupants from boiling alive. After waiting for instructions, we were shown in to see the chief of police himself. He was a nice man I suppose. A little bit long in the tooth and not really imposing enough to be a senior African copper, but he listened attentively to the immigration officer before holding out his hand for my paperwork. His English was rudimentary, so Alex acted as unofficial interpreter. Even he looked sweaty and flustered at the rigmarole.

Ten minutes passed in silence broken only by the buzzing of innumerable flies and the police chief laboriously went through my passport and the letters of support. If he couldn't speak English, I wasn't sure how he was reading English, but kept my doubts to myself. All I wanted was to find a bar somewhere and have an ice cold beer.

Eventually the policeman spoke. He directed his remarks to Alex and that worthy shrugged as he translated them for my benefit.

"He says that he cannot make this decision himself," that sounded wearyingly familiar, "so we must go and see the governor."

Our little party duly increased by the presence of the chief of police, we headed across to the governor's mansion where at least the fans seemed more efficient. After waiting for fifteen minutes or so, we were called and trooped in to a large, airy office where governor Jose Laissone Chissale indicated that due to my advanced age (he didn't actually put it like that) I should sit while my three companions should stand behind me. Once again I handed over my papers and studied the man carefully as he read slowly through them. Unlike my two former inquisitors, he was not in uniform but wore a light coloured safari suit and no shoes – slightly incongruous in the circumstances.

Once he had finished his perusal of the documents, I was asked to tell my story again and with Alex doing his interpreter act, I tried not to sound irritated or angry at being forced to repeat myself for the umpteenth time.

The Governor – his actual title was *Administrador Distrital* listened intently and I tried to read what he was thinking, but he kept his face impassive. When I spluttered to a stop, he suddenly stood up and stepped around the desk. His round black face split into a beaming smile and in halting English, he bade me welcome to Mozambique. I was more than a little taken aback at this sudden extreme change of tack, but I shook his hand and endured a hot and sweaty hug before he directed Alex to take photographs of us all.

"You will be a great credit to my country." I was told. "If at any time you need help along the way, contact me and I will do what I can to assist."

He was genuine too. Before I left his office, he gave me another hug and handed me his business card with further instructions to 'call me at any time of day and night.'

The walk back to the immigration office and my pack was conducted in a totally different atmosphere to the rest of the morning. My companions chattered garrulously in a mixture of languages, while I thought to myself how incredibly unpredictable life can be in rural Africa.

The chief of police solemnly shook my hand when we left him and the immigration officer banged his stamp down on my passport with great ceremony. Other immigration officers were called and my story was told again, this time in the local dialect and not by me. I listened impassively, trying hard not to look too smug.

Outside once more in that blistering sun, I hefted my pack and told Alex that it was 'beer time or bust.' As a Rastafarian, he didn't touch alcohol, but he was equally hot and sweaty, so off we went along the dusty streets of Zumbu to find a bar. I also needed somewhere to stay that night. The day had already provided enough drama and I didn't want to walk on just yet. Besides, I wanted to cross the Zambezi before going any further. After long emailed discussions with local people before I left England, I had decided that although the southern shoreline of Cabora Bassa contained a lot less in the way of wild life, it offered considerably easier walking as most of it was flat. The northern bank appeared very rocky and mountainous, so the decision was easily made, but I needed a boat to get me across the river.

Alex seemed sure that I would be able to hire a 'taxi' to get me across the following day, so we continued cheerfully down the long main street of Zumbu.

The first lodge we came to wanted to charge me twenty kwacha for a cell-like room with two beds in it and no access to either a loo or running water. As I had paid slightly less than that for my airy *en suite* bedroom at the Feira Lodge, I turned it down and the owner of the place merely shrugged and assured Alex that the vacancy would soon be filled.

The next establishment on offer had its own already well attended bar and that made me feel better, but after showing us a comfortable looking room and explaining the facilities on offer for a mere fifteen kwacha, the proprietor smilingly told us that he was 'full up.'

Feeling somewhat peeved at the waste of time, I went into a courtyard with my tame Rasta and we sat at a table beneath a large sun umbrella while a beer was brought for me and a coke for Alex. They were both icy cold and I sighed with pleasure as the balm slid down my throat.

Suddenly we were approached from inside the establishment by the owner, a thin, mixed-race young man who introduced himself as George.

"That is my real name," he explained, "but around here I am known as Georgito. I gather you are looking for somewhere to sleep."

I agreed that I was and he gestured to a patch of ground beside a reed fence that he said was his camping area.

"You can sleep there for five kwacha."

It wasn't what I wanted but it was too hot to keep walking, so I wearily agreed. Georgito sat down at our table and he and Alex were soon deep in conversation. I had no idea what they were talking about, but from Alex's gestures and Georgito's occasional admiring glances in my direction, guessed that they were discussing my trip. Another beer was called for and Alex turned to me.

"Our friend here tells me that he owns a hunting camp across the river and you are welcome to sleep there without payment if you like. He will even provide us with a boat to get across."

It seemed too good to be true and I looked at Georgito who grinned broadly, displaying alarmingly crooked and discoloured teeth.

"I am well known throughout the Zambezi area," He told me proudly. "On the other side, there is a small hunting road that travels for a long way beside the river so you should make good progress. If you find yourself in trouble along the way, ask that a message be sent to Georgito from Zumbu."

That was the second such offer I had received that morning and despite the heat, I felt suddenly better.

I asked Georgito a few questions about lake Cabora Bassa and he seemed to be familiar with much of it so I listened intently to his advice. I was dreading the gorge below the dam wall, as that had been the obstacle that shattered David Livingstone's dreams and ultimately broke his heart. It was said to be cruel countryside and I had fairly horrific memories of the gorges below Victoria Falls as well as the picturesque Mupata Gorge to fuel my worries. Both had tried hard to kill me and Cabora Bassa was looming ever larger among my anxieties.

"I don't know that gorge," Georgito admitted, "but on the lake, you will find a kapenta fisherman known as Mawaya. He will know how to tackle the gorge. Like me, he is well known throughout Mozambique and he is a mzungu, so will be happy to assist."

That was the first occasion on which I heard mention of a man who was to become a friend and have a huge bearing on the ultimate success of my journey.

Sitting beneath a very basic thatched shelter that evening, I looked across at the bright lights of Zumbu and reflected on the day.

Georgito had been as good as his word and supplied us with a banana boat and driver that took me across to the hunting camp – it obviously hadn't been used in years – and then ferried Alex back to Zambia.

I was sorry to bid farewell to my Rastafarian friend. Alex had helped enormously and it was all out of the goodness of his heart. Over the telephone, he had introduced me to his wife Maria and promised me that they would both be praying for me over the next few months.

"You have a long way to go Madala." He said as he enveloped me in a hug. "Maria and I will be with you in spirit and we will be here for you when you return in triumph."

Someone had faith in me even if my own self-belief was taking a battering. I waved Alex off and as the little vessel puttered away, was amazed to see that the big fellow had dissolved into tears. Perhaps he didn't have as much faith in me as I had thought or perhaps he just knew something that I didn't.

That was a sobering thought.

Source of the Zambezi

Sioma Ngonye Falls

Happy party leaving Siavonga. Nick Taylor, Audrey McGeorge, Zara Taylor, Alexis Phiri and myself.

Immigration Ladies, Ingrid and Miriam at Luangwa

Zumbu officialdom - and me

Farewell to Rasta Alex

Lunch at Chiawa Village

Mopani Forest - easy to get oneself lost.

Typical Cabora Bassa shoreline

Off on the Livingstone Trail. Isiah, Mawaya, myself, Moffat and Ronnie.

Watched by locals, I make an offering to the Spirits.

Johan and I trying to keep warm

CHAPTER FIVE
(An Embarrassing Mistake)

Panyame Hunting Camp was known as Kafukudze among locals and was a far cry indeed from the rickety little establishment of Georgito's opposite Zumbu. I had followed what was obviously a hunting road running parallel to the river and on my third evening, met up with a shooting party in a big land cruiser. They supplied me with much needed water and told me that I was about ten kilometres from the camp. I posed for pictures with a couple of cheerful American clients and promised to tell them all about my little adventure when I saw them the following day.

The visitors' part of Panyame was very luxurious, but I was asked to stay in staff quarters where I shared a tent with Johan Uys, a cheerful farming lad from Cape Agulhas on the southernmost tip of Africa and a coloured man from Harare called Rodney Emmanuel. They were lovely fellows and I spent two days in their company before moving on toward another hunting camp, owned by the same company and called Mbadzi. At Panyame I met Bryn Joliffe who asked whether I was any relation to Graeme Lemon. I assured him that I was and he told me that Rob Oostindien who was one of the hunters in camp had actually been at school with my son.

Johan was doing a hunting apprenticeship with the company while Rodney was in charge of the camp vehicles, so they were both pretty busy, but we spent our evenings sitting in the shade of huge trees and looking out on the headwaters of Lake Cabora Bassa. I saw no sign of the American clients, which was a pity but I had plenty of things to do.

Wandering around the camp in the company of a watchful guard were a young elephant and a buffalo of similar age. They had obviously been rescued after a hunt and seemed quite at home in camp. The only problem to my mind was they had both outgrown babyhood, were completely accustomed to being with people and were incredibly strong and boisterous in their play. Inevitably one or other would damage somebody and then they would doubtless be put down. I would have liked to chat with camp manager Greg Vegassi about their future, but I didn't get to see him again.

Panyame provided a pleasant interlude in my walk, but I left the place feeling vaguely dissatisfied. There was so much more I would have liked to find out – not least what sort of wild life remained in the area to be hunted – but apart from Johan and Rodney, nobody seemed in the slightest bit interested in talking with me.

But as I said, it had been a pleasant interlude and when I pulled out of camp early one May morning, I felt a little thrill that I would now be walking around the great lake of Cabora Bassa – a body of water I knew nothing about but presumed would be very similar to Lake Kariba.

I was horribly wrong and little did I know it, but I was about to make one of the most embarrassing mistakes of my life.

* * *

I wasn't sorry to leave the hunting area. I had seen very few signs of wild life, so when villages started to appear beside the track I was following, I felt myself relax and began to enjoy the walk.

As had been the case in Zambia, the first people to notice me were always the children, but now instead of shrill 'How are yous' being hurled at me from both sides of the road, it was equally shrill 'Bom dias.'

Responding in kind, I somewhat sadly reflected that although I had a Portuguese phrase book in my pack, I hadn't really studied it, which meant that 'Bom dia' and 'obrigardo' (Thank you) were about the sum total of my Portuguese vocabulary. This became a problem when I arrived in a sprawling village beside the broad Panyame River. I needed to get across and although there were a number of dug outs on the river I didn't have a clue how to ask for a lift. My English met with a total lack of understanding and the people I approached merely shrugged and jabbered back at me in quick fire Portuguese.

At last I found a thick-set fellow who seemed to understand and he threw my pack into his canoe before gesturing to me to sit on the gunwale. That was a first for me as I normally made myself as comfortable as possible on the floor of a boat, but as he was paddling from the opposite gunwale, I had little choice in the matter. It was difficult to relax, but eventually we grounded on the far bank and I gave the boatmen a few meticais as my thank you.

His hitherto serious mien changed remarkably. A huge grin split his face and he shook my hand with enthusiasm. I couldn't help wondering just how much I had given him. Kwacha had been readily acceptable until then and I had concentrated on getting rid of my remaining Zambian cash, but from here on I would be using the Mozambique currency and I wasn't really sure about it at that stage.

But it didn't matter. I followed a tiny path into the Mopani scrub and was relieved to be back on the road again. I was still some kilometres from the edge of the lake, but edged myself ever closer by taking any path or track that seemed to be going in the right direction. Not very scientific I know, but it worked.

That evening, I camped beside the lake and enjoyed a spectacular sunset. A wide variety of water birds added their clamour to the evening ambience and I felt very much at peace, despite aching muscles. The mosquitoes were bad however and I wasted little time in getting my net up and curling my body to accommodate it. For all the discomfort involved, it felt good to sleep beside a large stretch of water again and I fell asleep, watching for shooting stars and satellites in that glorious night sky.

My immediate goal was the hunting camp at Mbadzi, but sticking close to the lake shore made for difficult walking. Lake Kariba is a far older lake and the shoreline has had time to form beaches and grasslands that are easy to walk across, but Cabora Bassa seemed to be still trying to find its way and there were many deep, rocky inlets that took me hours to get around. It would doubtless have been easier to go inland and find a path, but I was in a stubborn frame of mind for some reason. So it was that I walked on my chosen route, despite suffering a number of falls on rocks and sitting down hard in a muddy puddle that left me feeling very uncomfortable until the mud dried.

The day was terribly hot and I could feel sweat streaming off me with the exertion, so it was with some relief that I staggered into a small fishing camp around midday. The fishermen looked vaguely guilty and gave the impression that they were up to no good, but as none of them could speak English, conversation was difficult and I soon left them to their own devices.

The heat was getting to me however and it was a relief to sit down beneath a big Mopani tree that offered a modicum of shade. I was dropping off to sleep when shrill laughter caught my attention. A group of village women were fishing in the shallows by dragging mosquito nets through the water and scooping up hundreds of fingerlings. Once again I felt a feeling of despair. What future does the inland fishing industry have in rural Africa?

Mosquito nets were undoubtedly needed in this part of Mozambique. Mossies along the lake were appallingly aggressive. I have lived much of my life among the horrible little creatures and they invariably come out at night or when the weather is cooler, but these Cabora Bassa types were twenty-four hour workers. Whenever I stopped, no matter how hot it was, large and obviously well fed mosquitoes would descend upon every square millimetre of exposed skin. I slept in the bush, so what it must have been like in the villages, I dreaded to think, yet here were obviously donated mosquito nets being used to decimate the fish population.

There are times when I wish those in charge of the various Aid agencies would walk with me through rural Africa. That way they could see just how misplaced their efforts are. Donated clothing ends up on market stalls, food supplies are usually hijacked by local entrepreneurs and sold on, while mosquito nets are used for fishing.

While I was meditating on life beneath my tree, I was suddenly approached by a cross-eyed young man who hesitantly introduced himself as Chawala Tolo. Pointing to his mouth, he was obviously asking me whether I was hungry, so I nodded vigorously. With a tremulous half smile, he hoisted my pack on to one shoulder and I accompanied him to a rude hut among the trees, where he gave me a meal of nshima (ncima in Mozambique but pronounced the same way) and inevitably, dried fish. The ncima was lumpy and tasted rancid while the fish wasn't much better, so I prayed that my stomach would handle it. However, Tolo's gesture was a kind one and I wandered on feeling slightly more cheerful about everything.

In Zambia, every villager I came across had been friendly and hospitable, but here in Mozambique – and it could well have been due to the language barrier – they were far more reserved. Not unfriendly by any means and 'bom dias' rang through the forest wherever I went, but few of them volunteered to talk or carry my pack.

Chawala Tolo was the first exception to this and I went on my way feeling considerably better about life.

In another very basic camp where three men and their children were gutting and scaling a vast pile of fish, I met up with a rotund individual who I think told me that his name was Fletcher. It was probably something Portuguese, but I addressed him as Fletch and he didn't seem to mind. When he learned that I was heading for Mbadzi, he offered to guide me – an offer gratefully accepted. We walked slowly to a village called Nyakasadza and from there, Fletch led me deep into Mopani forest and away from the lake. I was doubtful and asked where we were going and he smilingly announced that he knew a man with a car who would be happy to take me to Mbadzi for a fee.

Feeling that I had wasted a lot of time and a huge amount of energy on a fruitless bit of walking, I rounded on Fletch and told him that I would camp where I was and resume my walk in the morning. He shrugged non committedly and assured me that he would meet me at six and show me the way to a road that led directly to Mbadzi.

After another night battling marauding mosquitoes, I was at the agreed rendezvous point at six, but an hour later, gave up on Fletch and resumed my walk. Perhaps foolishly I continued inland, following a narrow track that wound its way through a vast Mopani forest. I kept an eye on the path of the sun and tried to ensure that I was going east, but Mopani trees are all alike and in such forest, it is often difficult to concentrate on direction. I should have used my compass I suppose, but I was hot and sweaty and had no idea that anything was wrong.

The morning wore on and in one little village, I found a man who spoke reasonable English. When I asked him how far I was from Mbadzi, he told me that it was about twenty-eight kilometres away and pointed back in the direction I had come from. That was serious and I felt that he had to have it wrong. I explained that Mbadzi was a hunting camp belonging to Safaris de Mozambique and his expression lightened. He told me there was just such a camp about twenty kilometres 'across the swamp.'

Said swamp was a vast area of papyrus reeds and water that I gazed at with much trepidation. My village linguist assured me that for twenty American dollars he would provide me with a boat and two escorts who would not only take me across the swamp, but then carry my pack to the hunting camp. I beat him down to ten dollars and half an hour later, we set off.

There were hippo among the reeds as well as a huge assortment of water birds and it was a very pleasant interlude in what had until then been an exhausting day. My escorts, Christopher (it was actually more Portuguese than that) and Anderson paddled expertly and were completely unphased when a pod of hippo erupted in panicked confusion almost beneath the boat. Neither of them could speak English, so I was unable to question them, but they were pleasant enough and when we landed at a small jetty, Christopher cheerfully picked up my pack and started off at a brisk walk. Yelling after him, I pantomimed that he was going too fast for me and we slowed to a reasonable pace. I confess to feeling vaguely smug when he started to wilt after a kilometre or so and handed the pack over to his smaller companion.

We were following what looked like a hunters' road again and it went on and on and on and on. Packless and with only a water bottle and my walking pole to encumber me, I was wilting too and after a while, my mind switched off and I walked automatically. No longer did I gaze around me with interest; no longer did I try to identify bird calls or animal spoor in the dusty earth - I just pushed myself on and concentrated on putting one foot in front of the other.

My heart was bursting and my legs felt like rubber when I suddenly saw a building through the trees and realised that we had made it. We had been walking for a good two hours in blistering heat and had covered far more kilometres than I normally did in an entire day, but somehow I had managed to stay upright. With a sudden spring in my step, I hurried toward the building which was obviously a workshop. A man working in the bowels of a land cruiser straightened slowly and looked at me with obvious astonishment.

"I didn't think we had looked after you that well," It was Rodney and I wondered what he was doing at Mbadzi.

At my question, he paused a moment then burst into raucous laughter.

"This isn't Mbadzi David. This is Panyame where you left us three days ago."

I felt as though I had walked into a wall. I had pushed myself to the absolute limit for three whole days and was back where I started. Somehow I had walked in a vast circle, probably losing my way in the Mopani forest and coming back on myself. Yet it didn't seem possible. I would have had to cross the Panyame River to get back here and although I had crossed that huge swamp, there had been no sign of a river. None of it made sense and having thanked my two porters – they seemed as bewildered as I was – I went with Rodney to have lunch in the staff mess tent. He couldn't stop laughing.

"Now you will have to write about us," He chortled. "We will play a big part in your book and I want to read it."

I can't remember what we had for lunch, but I spent most of it shaking my head at my own idiocy, while Rodney and Johan teased me gently. How on earth could I have made such a stupidly embarrassing mistake? Fortunately for me, Johan was driving to Mbadzi that afternoon and offered to take me along – an offer I readily accepted. After covering forty odd hard kilometres in search of the place, I felt I deserved a bit of comfortable travel.

* * *

The impala ram staggered, took a pace forward and fell with his nose in the dust.

Johan had told me that he needed to shoot something for camp rations at Mbadzi and while I admired the way, he had dispatched the young male, I couldn't help feeling sad at the demise of a fine animal. I have shot for the pot many times in the past, but it is always a tragedy to see lovely antelope eyes go dim, just so that people can eat.

The journey to Mbadzi took us over four hours and the truck had to be dug out of drifts at least three times before we reached our destination. The road wound well inland and there was little water to be seen, so I thanked my stars that I had chosen a route beside the lake – even if it had led to considerable embarrassment.

The camp itself was situated at the head of a deep inlet and sitting on the veranda of the main building, I reflected that the view was one of the most heart-achingly beautiful vistas I had encountered in a lifetime of wandering. Calm blue water, the varying greens of the surrounding bush and great rocky outcrops on either side were enough to soothe the most troubled of souls.

I stayed in that enchanted spot for two days. Johan and I gorged ourselves on fresh impala steaks and talked late into the night. He didn't feel that he would make a career out of hunting, but was enjoying bush life and the experience.

"I am a farmer at heart and will eventually return to help my Father," He told me simply. "It will be wonderful to go home."

I left Mbadzi to the good wishes of the staff and felt a wrench at leaving genuinely nice people. Since then, Johan Uys has indeed returned to the family farm on Cape Agulhas and Rodney Emmanuel has gone back to Harare, where I trust he is doing as well as anyone can do in modern Zimbabwe.

I made steady progress along the lake shore, but another big difference between Cabora Bassa and Lake Kariba was the shallowness of the water. In Kariba, it was always easy to fill up a water container or cooking pot by dipping it into the shallows, but here, I often needed to walk hundreds of metres off shore before the water was deep enough. Every step churned up the mud too, so eventually I decided that washing was a huge waste of time and energy. For eleven days, I went without a bath and must have smelled pretty bad at the end of it.

I was still sticking as closely as possible to Cabora Bassa shoreline, but quite apart from the extra distance that gave me to walk, it made for difficult going over rocky ground and after a number of falls, I was covered in cuts and grazes. My handkerchiefs were sodden from mopping away blood and I felt very down as I drew closer to the Musengezi River which was my next objective. I was not enjoying myself, but the kilometres were falling away behind me and as always, I met some wonderful people in the villages.

CHAPTER SIX
(Lake Shore Walking)

Communication with the locals was particularly difficult in this part of Cabora Bassa and in many villages, nobody was able to speak English or Portuguese so that my by now, well-thumbed phrase book was redundant. I was usually able to ask for water, but that was all, although on a few occasions, villagers pressed cassava or sweet potatoes into my hands when I left them.

At a huge, sprawling conurbation called Donga Camp, I was fortunate to meet up with a young man called Kanyamazulu – it means 'All the Animals are Ours' - who spoke reasonable English and in my relief to actually converse again, I probably became quite garrulous. He guided me onward and pointed out a well-defined path for the following day. It was quite far from water, but he assured me that it would take me right through to the Musengezi and it would only take me two days to get there. I was carrying two and a half litres of water at this stage and as I still wasn't bathing, felt that I could probably eke it out to last forty-eight hours.

I was in a very strange frame of mind during this period of my walk. I didn't want it to end, but at the same time I longed to reach the finish. It meant that I pushed myself to the limit of my physical capabilities instead of ambling along and enjoying my wild surroundings. Physically I felt terribly weary and my leg muscles ached more than they had ached since that incredibly strong young man, Kaluka Kaluka had walked with my pack on his bicycle some fifteen hard kilometres into Limilunga. And that had been a long time previously.

On the other hand, the countryside I was passing through was pretty drab and didn't offer much incentive for dawdling. When I wasn't climbing over cursed rocks, I was walking through Mopani woodland and much as I love those gaunt forest giants, their very uniformity – they are all thick and straight – tended to numb the mind at times – and of course made it easy to get lost as I had already proved to myself.

The daytime heat was also taking its toll and I knew it wasn't doing me any good. Every evening when I took my shirt off, it had a thin crust of dried salt on the back. I knew I couldn't afford to lose the stuff at that rate, but didn't know what I could do about it. This was mid-winter and the nights were sometimes chilly but during the day, the temperatures would rocket and half way through the afternoon, would be well into the forties. That was another reason that I needed to get the walk over with. After two bouts of malaria and losing all my front teeth at the end of the first leg, I was beginning to wonder whether my ancient frame would stand up to the punishment I was inflicting upon it. I was enjoying myself – at least I felt I probably was – but I needed to reach my ultimate goal before my strength gave out.

So it was that I wandered along, not only aching in every pore of my being, but in a very confused and tormented mental state as well. At times I tried to occupy my mind by counting my steps as I went along, but all too often I lost count and annoyed myself.

Fundungwe Village was another of those places where the path I was following suddenly petered out and I was faced with the prospect of skirting a very large inlet. As I stood wondering whether to tackle the way ahead or camp for the night, a little fellow called Hakim Moffat offered in sign language to take me across in his tiny little canoe. That little act of kindness saved me a good two hours and although we couldn't communicate with each other, a shared handshake and mutual smiles said it all.

On another occasion, I passed a pretty little pan that offered plentiful shade as well as abundant water, but it was early in the day, so a little reluctantly I walked on. Two long, dusty kilometres later, that little water hole seemed an infinitely desirable place to be and with a grunt of self-disgust, I turned around and walked back to spend a restful day watching Egyptian geese and doing absolutely nothing.

In Kaburu Village, I met up with Chief Makuni, a jovial soul dressed in torn clothing, but wearing a hat and carrying a carved swagger stick to denote his chiefly status. Headman Newman was called in as interpreter and after all my details, including passport number had been entered in the village diary, the chief and I had a long talk. He told me that I was twenty-five kilometres from Kabale village where I could get a canoe across the Musengezi. That was a blow as I had hoped to reach the river that day, but there was nothing for it but to plod on.

The chief wasn't having that however and called on a young, fit looking man called Magongwane to escort me to Kabale with my pack on the back of his bicycle. It was wonderful to walk unencumbered again, but Magongwane soon became bored with pushing his bike beside me. Mounting his faithful njinga, he disappeared up a long, dusty road, leaving me plodding along behind. I could only marvel at how trusting I had become. I had handed all my worldly goods to a complete stranger who had disappeared into the wilds of Africa – all for a few hours of relatively comfortable walking.

I was in a quandary when I came to a fork in the road however. I searched the surface for Magongwane's tyre tracks, but as bicycles were the main form of transport in that area, there were literally hundreds of cycle tracks on each road. While I was wondering which way to go, a scotch cart hove into view with a family and their belongings piled high. The driver indicated the way to Kabale and invited me to climb aboard, but I declined politely. The cart was drawn by two oxen who looked so old, thin and worn that I felt sure I would arrive at my destination far quicker on my own two feet.

So it proved, but I walked through most of the afternoon and coming into a large village that had to be Kabale, I wondered how to find Magongwane and my pack. I need not have worried. My pack had been delivered to the headman Moses' house and I felt a sense of relief that my trust in the young man had not been misplaced. I left a generous token of my gratitude for him at the local store.

Moses made me welcome and told me that Kabale was the largest village in the province and held between nine hundred and a thousand souls. He smilingly explained that he could not keep up with the pregnancies, so the figure was only approximate. He took his duties seriously though and dressed very smartly to do his evening rounds of the village. I couldn't help contrasting his suave be-suited appearance with my own tattered and dirty look, so as soon as I was able to, I gave myself a good bath.

I met a lot of people in Kabale and a few of them spoke excellent English. One such was a very sweet lady called Agnes, who hailed from my own home town of Marondera in Zimbabwe. She was visiting relatives in Kabale and we enjoyed a long chat and memories of home.

I could cheerfully have stayed a week in that big, busy village, but all too soon it was time to move on and cross the mighty Musengezi. The evening before I left, Angela brought her nephew Abraham across with the news that he would take me in his boat, but only for twenty US dollars. The Musengezi is a large river, but I didn't think it was that large, so eventually we compromised on ten dollars – still somewhat expensive in my eyes. Abraham wanted payment in advance, but I declined and was proved right when he failed to turn up at the jetty next morning.

Eventually a fellow calling himself Chico arrived with a young boy and agreed to take me across in his banana boat. I could pay him in meticais rather than dollars too, so that made me feel better.

In Zambia, few village officials had checked my papers or made serious enquiries as to my intentions, but in most Mozambican villages, I was taken to see the headman or village clerk and my details were faithfully recorded. I wondered if this was a legacy from the cruel civil war that had ravaged the country a few years previously. It was sometimes wearying when I was tired, hot and irritable, but I could see the sense in it and if anything, had happened to me, at least people would have been able to find out what progress I had made.

I was following a road for much of the time. I was repeatedly told that it went all the way to Tsongo, which was apparently a large centre on the lake shore, although I never actually found it. At one stage I reflected that I hadn't seen the lake in days and was heartily sick of carrying water as well as my pack.

When I was too weary to continue, I would get off the road to camp in the bush and sleep beneath the stars, usually feeling that I had surely the nicest bedroom ceiling in the world. I think it was shortly after crossing the Musengezi that on one particular evening, I saw the largest meteorite that I have ever seen. It lit up the night sky, seeming to start fairly low in the heavens and getting brighter as it went. It must have been in sight for at least four or five seconds and as the star was heading due east, I took that as an omen of success in my venture and slept well for the rest of the night.

The people I met were still very friendly even though we couldn't really converse with each other. On one occasion, an old gentleman was driving his scotch cart in the opposite direction to me and for the life of me, I couldn't remember my 'bom dias.' I mumbled something in English and he solemnly raised his hat to greet me with, "Cool Man."

It seemed that twenty-first century idiom had reached even the innermost portals of Mozambique.

One of the few 'luxuries' I had allowed myself to carry throughout the walk was a few sticks of biltong, the dried meat staple of Africa. These I cut into bite-sized portions, which I allowed myself to chew every few days. Now as a result – I presume - of the intense heat, my remaining biltong was beginning to go mouldy. I wasn't going to throw it out though and continued to chew when I felt the need. What with mouldy biltong and muddy water, I suppose it was a wonder that my stomach didn't give me far more trouble than it actually did.

The further down the lake I trudged, the worse the mosquitoes became. When I packed up camp in the mornings, they would fly around me in a dense cloud and throughout the day I would be subject to their depredations. I took my deltaprim prophylactic every Sunday and just prayed that the malaria would keep away. As it was, my first aid sessions were becoming more frequent as I pushed myself along and I had a strange lump on the side of my right instep that scared me a little. It was hard and didn't hurt but seemed to be getting ever larger and redder. The prospect of digging into it with my knife did not appeal in the slightest!

On my forty-second day since leaving Siavonga, I started wading across a small river, but when the water came up over my shorts, I turned back. I didn't fancy a ducking even though I needed a bath. Taking my boots off I received a shock when a dead fish dropped out of the right one. It wasn't a small fish either and how it had found its way into my footwear I couldn't imagine but there it was. Strange things happen to wanderers in Africa.

That evening I looked back on my progress and felt quite pleased with myself. I was well over half way down the lake and at night could see the lights of kapenta rigs out on the water. I have always cursed those lights as spoiling the joys of an African night, but here they made me feel vaguely nostalgic. They brought memories of lazy days on Lake Kariba as well as all my adventures on that particular piece of water.

Here though was a different stretch of water and thoughts of the Cabora Bassa gorge began intruding whenever I felt good. That gorge had foiled David Livingstone in his plans to create a trading route to the interior and ultimately it had broken his heart. I hadn't seen the gorge and didn't know what it looked like, but memories of the torment and pain I had suffered in previous gorges, made the prospect of going through it all over again an unappetising one.

But that was still a few weeks away, so I banished the doubts as well as I could and kept walking.

CHAPTER SEVEN
(The Road to Casindira)

I had set myself a brutal pace all morning and my legs were beginning to ache. The previous evening, I had rearranged my kit, putting the heavy food bag with two water bottles in the upper half of the pack in the hope that it would ease the enormous strain on my back. For a while it had made a difference. Now the pain was back and I looked around for somewhere to camp.

I was moving through more Mopani woodland now and spotting a burly man cutting wood not far from the path I was using, I called out a slightly less than enthusiastic, "Bom dia."

"Good morning," Was his surprising reply. "Where are you going?"

Simba Mabwe was a Zimbabwean from Mzarabani and with an enthusiastic heave, swung my pack on to his shoulders and led me down a narrow path to his home at Ndewe village. There I was introduced to the entire Mabwe clan and my walk through this remote corner of Africa was explained by my new friend. His wife – she was actually his girlfriend as he cheerfully admitted to having a wife in Harare – Priscilla immediately set about preparing a meal, while Simba showed me around a sprawling village.

"We are traders," He explained. "We bring our scotch carts down the escarpment every couple of months. We buy fish and clothing, then take it back to Mzarabani and sell it in the markets."

There were three well laden scotch carts outside Simba's hut and he went on to tell me that they were leaving for Zim the following day. He insisted that I stayed the night and when I demurred, pointing out that I would be in the way of their preparations for leaving, he laughed uproariously.

"We will leave when we are ready," He told me. "Only you white people start off early. We will be travelling for three to four days, so there is no hurry to get going."

I rather envied them their leisurely way of travel.

Brunch was a cheerful affair, frequently interrupted by visitors, obviously wanting to see the strange mzungu, who had emerged from the forest. Simba explained his relationship with each of them but I soon lost track. Apart from Priscilla, there were three other ladies, named Lorraine, Cecilia and Dorothy, their very English names seeming vaguely out of place in such a wild corner of Mozambique. They all made much of me though and it was nice to be the centre of attention.

My pleasure was enhanced when water was heated for me to bathe and I emerged from the roofless bathing hut, clean, shaved and feeling considerably better. Priscilla took my filthy clothes away to wash and somewhat to my surprise, they were returned that evening, not only smelling good, but freshly ironed. Irons in this part of undeveloped Africa seemed incongruous somehow.

The rest of the day passed in truly African style. The women busied themselves, washing, cleaning and preparing food, while the men sat around in the shade, discussing a variety of subjects. In my honour I presume, they spoke in English and I listened intently. A pack of worn playing cards was produced and Simba sat opposite his brother Cosmos, playing a game that I could neither understand nor follow While they were thus engaged, I was approached by a man called Wilson Shaya who told me that he had been in the British South Africa Police of Rhodesia and then the Zimbabwe Republic Police. So had I and we reminisced for a while, but had been stationed in different sectors of the country, so found few memories in common.

A general election in Mozambique was due in a couple of months' time and this aroused a great deal of interest among these Zimbabweans. If there was a new government, how would it affect their trading life? Would they need additional visas and permits to enter the country and would the cost of living rise?

As they seemed to travel back and forth through pretty desolate countryside and didn't bother with border formalities at Mzarabani, I didn't see how a change of government would really affect them, but I held my tongue. I was but a visitor.

It was pleasant to relax and feel the tension easing from my overtaxed muscles, but I had very little time to myself. All four of the women wanted to know how I lived in Britain. Did I have many children? Did I live in a big house like the wazungu of Harare, Tete and Maputo and did I eat sadza for my meals like any other African?

It was intriguing to realise that although they were well dressed and spoke excellent English, these ladies had absolutely no idea of the world outside their little domain. In the frenetic twenty-first century, I found this somehow comforting. At least the curses of civilisation hadn't reached here yet and I hoped they never would.

Dorothy asked if she could accompany me when I left, so I laughed and told her that she could but only if she carried my pack. She promised that she would and we all howled with mirth. She was a well-built girl, but the pack stood almost as tall as she did. I thought no more about it.

I went to bed that evening, having bade my cheerful hosts *bon voyage* and Simba promised to escort me out of the village at five the following morning.

"There is a road that will take you all the way to Matendere," He promised. "I will put you on to that so that you won't get lost."

Before leaving Britain, I had exchanged letters with a South African businessman named Doug Hensberg who seemed to have fingers in a number of Mozambican pies. He had promised to give me a few days off at his kapenta fishing camp and I had contacted him soon after entering Mozambique.

"Make for a place called Casindira," Was his advice over the telephone. "It is close to the Musengezi River and I will meet you there."

The only problem was that none of the locals I spoke with had ever heard of Casindira and I had no idea whether it was a village, a town or just a bush camp. Simba was no exception and advised me to ask again when I reached Matendere, itself apparently a large centre on the lake shore.

We set off on time the following morning and Simba carried my pack for the first three kilometres. Then he handed it back and we said our good byes. I was sorry to see him go as he had been a lovely character and with his family and their friendly kindness, had brought my aching frame back to life.

Wandering on, I found myself wading through a five hundred metre stretch of thick black mud and soon after getting through that, paused for breath and a scrape of my boots at the gateway to the Sabre Hills Safari Lodge. It would probably have been nice to go into the lodge, but a signpost told me that it was still two kilometres away and that would mean an extra two kays back, so I sat on my pack beside the track and smoked a contemplative pipe.

A call from further down the track interrupted my day dreaming and I turned to see Dorothy half running up a hill to catch up with me.

"You didn't wait for me," She panted. "When I woke up, they told me you had already left."

The previous day I had laughed off her offer to accompany me with an invitation to carry my pack, so I hadn't even given her a thought before leaving.

"I thought you would be going back to Zimbabwe with Simba and the family."

She shook her head.

"They are my friends, not my family. I live in Malawi and come here to buy fish."

Despite my threat to make her carry my pack, I wearily hoisted it onto my back again and we went on, Dorothy chattering away about her life and the many friends she had all over Africa.

"But I have never met anyone like you," Despite the pain in my shoulders, I couldn't help a little inward preening. "I want you to be my friend as well."

I assured her that would not be a problem and we walked companionably onward.

During my early days in Mozambique I had been surprised to find that a number of very basic villages seemed to have their own bank. Signs for the local banca were prominently displayed and it took me a while to learn that this denoted a store, rather than a financial institution. Orlando Village was another large one and the banca displayed an additional hoarding that advertised 'cold drinks' in English. We wandered in and Dorothy was obviously telling the lady behind the counter about me so that when I ordered two orange drinks, I was not allowed to pay for my own but the money was accepted for Dorothy's. We sat in the sun and chatted to villagers for a while, then Dorothy asked whether I would like some ground nuts. I thought she meant a bag of nuts to carry with me, but she took me to a large hut and introduced me to Amai Orlando, who was preparing a tray of groundnuts in their shells. I was handed a plateful and even without salt, they were delicious, the smoke of the fire having permeated the shells and imparted a lovely flavour. Perhaps I was just very hungry.

Whatever the case, the groundnuts were followed by ncima and fish and while Amai Orlando couldn't speak a word of English, she kept up a continuous barrage of questions, dutifully interpreted by Dorothy.

But it was time to move on and although Dorothy intended spending a few days with the Orlandos, she offered to carry my pack for a little while.

"I promised to do so yesterday," She smiled, but I held up my hands in horror.

"It is far too heavy for you, My Girl."

I must have sounded horribly patronising but a 'terribly British' upbringing meant that ladies were not allowed to perform heavy menial tasks – apart from cooking, ironing and cleaning of course.

But my tough little companion was insistent and we left Orlando Village to the good wishes of the residents and set off along a track that would apparently take me to Matendere Village. From there I was assured, it was but a short step to Casindira, although nobody could tell me what was at Casindira itself.

When she swung that awful pack up on to her shoulders, I saw Dorothy's knees buckle and she managed only a kilometre or so before telling me that she had to get back. I gave her a hug, thanked her for her company and complimented her on her strength. She seemed concerned for my welfare, but I had filled my water containers at Orlando and assured her that I would find a camp somewhere and be quite comfortable.

She did not seem convinced and when a large, villainous-looking man came up behind us, she engaged him in conversation, his glances at me confirming that I was the topic of discussion.

"This man will show you the way," She beamed at me. "He comes from the Congo so can even speak a little English."

We hugged again and parted but if Dorothy Muzongolo ever reads this narrative, she will be proud to know that she is and always will be the only female to carry that enormous pack of mine. She really made my day.

So off I went again, my calves beginning to ache with the strain as I had been walking on and off for well over six hours. My new companion set a brisk pace and I soon found myself falling well behind. He strode on obliviously, but looked back at one point where the path we were following branched off. With a click of his tongue, he walked back and indicated that he would take the pack. His English was not good, but we managed to make ourselves understood in French, a language I had studied at school, a very long time previously.

It was mid-afternoon when we came out on the lake shore beside a wide, picturesque bay. My Congolese friend took me to a sturdily built reed house and showed me inside. Two other villainous looking fellows examined me with obvious suspicion, but one produced a plastic chair for me to sit on and a tin mug of water which I gratefully drank down.

After some discussion between the three of them, it was seemingly agreed that I could sleep with them on the floor of the house, but quite apart from their cut-throat appearance, the building was hot and claustrophobic. As with the Zambians, the Mozambicans seldom include windows in their architectural designs.

I told them that I needed fresh air and pointed to a small grove of trees, some hundred metres distant. I would sleep there and they seemed to understand, although they urged me to return that evening and eat with them. As I was leaving, I asked if I could borrow one of their chairs and they readily agreed, so off I went to my little grove where I set up a very comfortable camp.

It was amazing what difference a chair could make. I have spent much of my life wandering through the bush and have used trees, rocks and various oddments to sit on, but have never accustomed myself to the attendant discomfort. I cannot sit flat-footed on my haunches like the average African villager and all too often have sat on the ground rather than take advantage of what the locals regarded as comfortable seats.

A chair – even a cheap plastic one such as I was now using – added an extra dimension to comfort. Chairs were designed to accommodate bottoms and although my own bum was still there, it was only barely so. During the first part of my Zambezi Trek, it had virtually disappeared and any sort of sitting became acutely uncomfortable, but I had some of it back now and the joy of wedging my buttocks into the curves of a chair was truly indescribable.

As I watched the sun setting that evening, I sat beside my fire like Lord Ruddy Linoleum and couldn't help reflecting that I was a lucky man indeed. The scene before me was idyllic. The lake stretched, flat and calm into hazy mountains on the opposite bank. Water birds wheeled around each other in frenetic circles while others flew straight and true in large packs, obviously on their way home to distant roosting grounds. A Goliath heron stood tall in the shallows, his head poised to strike at any moment, while on a nearby tree, two fish eagles shrieked, their heads bending back and thrusting forward again, almost as though they were in some ritualistic dance. Behind them, a flat-topped mountain on the northern shoreline glowed blue through the haze of distance.

"It is the Mozambique Table Mountain," A village Elder had told me a few days previously and so vast was the hill itself that it was to stay with me for many more days.

Youngsters drove cattle, donkeys and goats up from the water, their shrill cries competing with the avian chorus. Women gathered water from the shallows and talked comfortably among themselves, while I sat beneath two big Mopani trees, comfortable, replete and happily weary. I knew I would sleep well in this enchanted spot.

I was on the road early the following morning, having returned my borrowed chair well before the sun rose. It was a Sunday and the weather was cool and invigorating, so I made excellent progress. It took me less than an hour to reach Matendere and although I felt like buying something to eat as a sort of Sunday treat, none of the shops along the main street were open. On I trudged and as I was leaving the village, a big fellow came out from a roadside hut.

"Where are you going?" He enquired in excellent English.

I told him and he really surprised me by asking whether I would like a cup of tea. In rural Africa, few people drink the stuff, while milk and sugar are far too precious to waste in a drink. However, the offer was obviously genuine, so I stepped inside and watched in further amazement as he boiled water on a little camping gas stove.

Inevitably I suppose, Edmore was from Zimbabwe and like the lovely Mabwe family, was a trader in various commodities, although he rarely went home.

"My friend, Charles Tyson does all the travelling," He told me. "You must meet him, as I think he is going to see Chief Casindira today."

Charles was another Zimbabwean and after we had enjoyed tea together – I supplied the milk powder and told them about Cowbell – he told me that he would accompany me that morning to ensure that I didn't get lost. At my query as to how far it was to Casindira, he laughed and said it was 'only about twenty-five kilometres.'

That was far in excess of my usual daily distance and it must have shown on my face as Charles went on with a big grin.

"Don't worry. I will carry your pack."

That was different and soon we were walking briskly along a wide, dusty road that seemed to wind its way further and further from the lake. I queried this with Charles and told him of my phobia with water, but he airily waved my doubts aside.

"This way we have to climb a little, but it cuts off many kilometres."

Having entrusted my belongings and my welfare to him, I had little choice but to follow where he led. The early morning cool quickly disappeared and soon the landscape around us was baking under that remorseless sun. The sky looked almost white and even without the pack on my shoulders, I could feel sweat pouring down my body. Charles' blistering early pace had fallen away somewhat. The road surface was covered in stretches of soft sand and every step tore at calf muscles and added to our sweaty discomfort. By midday, we were both moving very slowly, but suddenly the road came out in a sprawling waterside village. Grinning triumphantly, Charles led me to a large hut with vividly coloured markings on the wall. It was the home of the Chief himself and it was necessary to pay our respects to the Great Man before we went any further.

Chief Casindira was a thin, ascetic looking man who told me that his name was Geraldo Jose Gabriel and that he was King of the Casindira. He was dressed in a camouflage jacket and denim jeans, but limped on a foot that was heavily bandaged. The other was encased in a sturdy brown shoe and through Charles, the chief explained that he had fallen off his motor cycle a few days previously. After carefully noting down my details and questioning me to discover my plans, Chiefy told me that the place I was probably looking for was Casindira Lodge, where many wazungu liked to stay. He didn't know Doug Hensberg, but told me that he needed to visit the lodge himself and would have had me taken around in a boat, but the boat had broken down.

We had apparently walked past the entrance to the lodge some kilometres beforehand and my heart sank as I contemplated having to walk all the way back. The chief had other ideas however. Chattering away in the vernacular to Charles, an arrangement was apparently come to and my escort for the morning rose briskly to his feet.

"It is too far to walk back to the lodge in this heat," he told me, "so the Chief has suggested that I take you back there on a motor cycle."

There was one drawback to that. We didn't have a motor cycle and nor were there any in sight. I raised my eyebrows to Charles and he laughed.

"Chief Casindira is a wealthy man and he has many motor cycles, so we will borrow one and I will return it to him later."

A small motor bike was produced by a minion and I gazed at it somewhat askance before climbing on behind a laughing Charles. He was obviously enjoying himself and we clattered away in a cloud of black smoke while I clung on to my driver like a frightened fairy. The bike was too small and too overloaded to bank properly on corners and trying to balance that bulky pack was dangerously difficult, but somehow Charles kept us moving and we did at least make excellent progress. On three occasions, we toppled over in thick sand and I was forced to walk while Charles wrestled the little machine along, but in the middle of a very hot afternoon, the pair of us staggered into Casindira Lodge, a place of infinite beauty and charm.

Sitting on a step outside the main building was a white man and when I asked him where I could find the manager, he told me in a broad Cockney accent that he was the very man.

Thus I came to meet Barry Van der Maas who did indeed hail from the East End of London. I didn't know it at the time, but my Zambezi Walk was about to change for the more comfortable and take on a dramatic new format.

CHAPTER EIGHT
(Home Comforts)

It seemed an age since I had slept in a bed and I struggled to drop off that night. Barry and I had talked long into the evening and although he didn't know Doug Hensberg, he was confident that he could find out where he was.

"The white community in Mozambique is very small, particularly around the lake." He told me. "A few phone calls in the morning and we will dig him up."

Barry had been in Mozambique for a few years and told me that he loved the country. He seemed to have fingers in a lot of business pies and when I asked how he coped with the language problem, he laughed uproariously.

"Portuguese is fairly simple," he chuckled, "but in this place we have guests from all over the place, so I have picked up a smattering of many languages."

I can't remember how the subject came up, but Barry was passionate about a process known as Pyrolysis. I had never heard of it but he explained that it was the conversion of waste into what he called biochar –a form of very rich fertiliser – as well as electricity and diesel.

He went on to demonstrate with pamphlets and diagrams how the waste – and it could be any sort of rubbish – was burned without oxygen in huge machines that looked very expensive. When I mentioned this, he nodded.

"The basic machine costs in excess of ten million dollars," Barry sounded almost evangelical in his enthusiasm, "but to large corporations that is peanuts and they soon recoup it through developing their own electricity, diesel and building aggregates."

Apparently the machines were proving very popular in Australia and the Eastern bloc, but Barry wanted to see them in Africa and I could see his point. It was all very interesting but the costs involved seemed pretty astronomical to my feeble mind while the science of it all left me baffled.

But it had been an enjoyable evening and the following day I met

Charlie Stanger, the only other white person on the lodge staff. Charlie was the chief mechanic and general handyman, responsible for ensuring that everything worked to its best capacity.

He questioned me at length about my walk and plans before giving me lots of advice about who best to contact and where to go when I reached Tete. I wrote down numerous addresses and telephone numbers, but in the event, I followed none of his recommendations. However, that was due to circumstances rather than choice.

For a spectacularly built lodge overlooking the lake, Casindira had few visitors. Barry told me that business people from Tete came out for the occasional weekend, but generally the lodge was empty.

"So you can stay as long as you like," He smiled. "You are already a celebrity in these parts and I will put you in a nice cabin so that you can enjoy a bit of comfort for a change."

Comfortable the cabin certainly was and there was an open veranda, offering a stunning view across the lake. The night sky was very bright when I went to bed and I spent ten minutes or so just drinking in the pleasures of the moment.

One unexpected drawback to my quarters from my point of view though was the abundance of large mirrors. Almost automatically, I glanced at one of them and there was the skinny, crumpled old man I had seen two years previously in Siavonga. The sight did nothing for my morale.

Despite having a difficult night with the unexpected comfort with which I was surrounded, it was marvellous to get up in the morning and not have to worry about lifting up my pack. Instead, I made a leisurely pot of tea from the facilities provided, and drank it on the veranda while I thought about what I had achieved and what still remained to be done.

It was my forty sixth day 'on the road' and as far as I could estimate, I had less than five hundred kilometres to go. In the context of the walk, that did not seem much, but I knew there would be hard times ahead. I wasn't far from the end of the lake and that dreaded gorge was beginning to loom ever larger among my fears. I felt that once I was through that, life would become easier, but first I had to get it well behind me.

I needed a rest though and despite the luxury, didn't want to spend it in Casindira. Doug Hensberg had told me that he had a kapenta business on an island, but when I put this to Barry over breakfast of fresh fruit and coffee, he frowned.

"There are the Carlisles who run a few rigs from Manyerere Island," He mused. "Then there is a bigger concern on an island just beyond Manyerere. I will find out this morning I promise."

But before he did, I managed to raise Doug on my cell phone and having told me that he was 'out of the country,' he advised me to make my way to Mike Fynn's hunting camp that was a few kilometres East of Casindira.

"I will meet you there as soon as I can," He promised.

"Let me take you there by boat," Barry said with enthusiasm. "I could do with a ride out."

I had met Mike Fynn many years previously when I was a young copper on Kariba and I knew his brother Rob reasonably well. I felt it would be nice to meet up with the man again and talk about the 'good old days' but it was not to be.

That afternoon, Barry and I moved slowly down the shoreline, but not a sign of Mike's camp could we see. Doug had told me that it was on the edge of the lake, but if we passed it, then it must have been superbly camouflaged and I didn't want to cheat by covering too many kilometres on water rather than on foot.

"That is Manyerere island," Barry pointed to a large hill apparently jutting from the water some distance offshore. "The one just past it could be what you are looking for. I owe the Carlisles a visit, so let's go and see shall we?"

Changing course, he headed out into the lake and shortly afterwards, I met Doug and Margi Carlisle with their son Andy.

"I have heard about your walk," Doug told me gravely. "You must be a strong man indeed."

I had long since come to the conclusion that although my walk down the Zambezi was physically gruelling, the real strength needed for its completion had to be mental. There had been so many occasions when I had had to force myself into taking the next few steps and so many times when I had felt totally beaten.

I brushed off Doug's compliment and told him what I was looking for. He confirmed Barry's theory.

"Yes, Doug runs a big outfit on the next door island," He mused. "He isn't there at the moment though and I don't think he is due back for a week or two."

"Why don't you stay with us for a few days," Margi put in. "We don't have a spare bed, but you can sleep on cushions in the lounge."

I needed a rest so it seemed an excellent idea, particularly when in the course of conversation, Barry invited us all to come over and spend a night at Casindira. I probably looked a bit doubtful and he laughed.

"It won't cost you anything," He chided. "I owe these people and you are an honoured guest in any case."

So it was that the following day, I sat in another comfortable launch with the Carlisles and we wandered slowly around the edge of the lake, pulling into deep bays and inlets for some desultory fishing, while I gazed with considerable awe at the northern shoreline.

What a wise decision it had been to stick on the southern side. It might have been hard going at times, but its difficulties paled into insignificance when matched against the gaunt cliffs, crags and swamps that comprised the northern shore. It was spectacularly beautiful and apparently teeming with wild life, but it might well have polished me off, had I attempted to walk down it.

At Casindira we enjoyed an excellent dinner and I had a far better night than my first one. I suppose it was because I wasn't worrying about contacting the elusive Mr Hensberg and knew that I had another day or two of pleasant rest on Manyerere to give me strength for whatever lay ahead.

The Carlisles were a lovely family to be with too. Doug was a former soldier in the Rhodesian forces and we exchanged a few memories of those days, while Margi was a motherly lass, who churned out delicious meals and snacks on a weird looking outdoor stove. She made energy bars that tasted divine and when I complimented her, she promised that I would have a bag or three to take with me when I left.

Their son, Andy was a professional hunter enjoying a bit of leave and he helped Doug out with the necessary checking of rigs and crews during the night. I slept peacefully through their comings and goings and spent my time reading or wandering around their beautiful garden. The night before I was due to leave, a storm blew up on the lake and the rigs were confined to base. The water was still far too rough for comfortable travel the next morning, so I was given an extra day of peaceful rest.

I was sad when it was time to leave Manyerere, but I had a walk to complete. Andy dropped me back on to the mainland with admonitions to 'keep in touch hey.'

Armed with a couple of dozen energy bars, I hit the road once more. I was well into kapenta fishing country now and there were roads and traffic everywhere. Tractors threw up clouds of dust and many of the locals rode motor cycles of the sort that Charles had taken me to Casindira on. There were well-stocked roadside bancas everywhere and quite a few brick built houses. In fact, it was a totally different world to the one I had been walking through for so many weeks. People seemed less friendly than they had been further west and of course, there was still that awful language barrier.

One hot morning I was stumbling along when I distinctly felt a jolt inside my right sock. Puzzled, I sat down and took both my boot and my sock off. The big lump on my foot had burst, the sock was soaked with smelly fluid and the hole that was left in my foot was full of tiny black specks. None of these were moving, so I wasn't sure whether they were alive or not and to this day, I have no idea what caused that strange lump and why it had so suddenly burst. The hole in my foot took many weeks to heal over, so I had the additional worry of keeping it clean to avoid infection.

But bursting lumps on my foot were the least of my worries and for three days, I wandered eastward through this semi civilised part of Africa, not really enjoying myself. Although for the most part, I stuck to tracks travelling in vaguely the right direction, I still managed to get myself lost one very hot afternoon.

I was looking for the lake shore in the hope that I could find a nice place to camp, but every path I followed seemed to twist and turn in varying directions. I was hot, sweaty and frustrated when I asked a young man on a bicycle how to get to the lake.

Not surprisingly, he looked at me as though I had lost my marbles. With a bicycle, this was 'the lake' but on foot, I was merely confused and irritable. In halting English, he explained that I needed to go up a road that looked horribly steep. I needed to go downhill to reach the water, not up but it was too difficult to explain, so I thanked him and plodded along the road he had indicated.

It must have been close to two o'clock, uncomfortably hot and I was merely putting one foot in front of the other without thinking about anything when a motor cycle came down the hill towards me. A young white man was riding it and he stopped to see if I was okay.

"I am trying to find the edge of the lake," I told him wearily. "Some bloke back there sent me in this direction."

"He probably thought you were looking for other mzungus," Keith Goddard grinned. "You certainly won't find the lake up here, but come back and have a cup of tea or a cool drink. You look as though you can do with it."

I felt as though I could do with it too, so eased myself gingerly on to the rear seat of the motor bike and off we went, turning into a beautifully designed and obviously much loved garden surrounding a couple of houses. Wearily, but relieved to be there, I alighted from my precarious perch. Keith called for tea and we sat in comfortable garden chairs.

Like everyone else I had met, Keith had heard about the crazy geriatric walking the length of the Zambezi and he was interested in hearing of my travels. Before I started to tell him anything though, he smiled at me again.

"You were a great friend of John Wells and my dad, Roley Goddard, weren't you?"

I must have come close to spilling my tea. John and Roley had served in the BSAP with me and although Roley had died many years previously, John and I had remained friends until he also died. I still kept closely in touch with his daughter Debbie in Harare.

But Keith hadn't finished with his surprises.

"Do you remember my mom, Shirley?"

Of course I did. She had been married to both my friends and way back when we were all young and silly, the Wells', Goddards and Lemons had enjoyed many a weekend of partying in what was then Marandellas, where John and I were stationed. I had last seen her in England at John's funeral and Keith shook me to the core by telling me that Shirley was in the house behind us, enjoying an afternoon nap.

I know life is full of coincidences, but that really was taking things to extreme. I was pretty sure that Shirley still lived somewhere in the South of England and to meet up with her in the wilds of Mozambique was truly amazing. She seemed equally surprised when she emerged from her siesta and we spent hours catching up over innumerable cups of tea.

Of course it meant that I had to stay the night with Keith, his wife Justine and Shirley. Over supper, I asked Keith whether he knew of a way through the Cabora Bassa Gorge or even a way around it.

"Very few of us know that area," He said gravely. "It is very wild, but if anyone can tell you of a way through it is Mawaya Hougaard. His camp is only a few kilometres East of here, so you can be there in a day

'Tomorrow, let's speak to my boss, Judd Havnar who probably knows this end of the lake far better than I do."

I was becoming ever more curious to meet Mawaya Hougaard who I had first heard about from Georgito way back in Zumbu. He sounded quite a character.

The following day I was introduced to Judd Havnar, who was a tall, affable fellow, far younger than I expected him to be. He shook his head and looked grave when I asked him about walking through the gorge.

"Downstream from the wall, you can probably get through," he said, "but above the wall itself you haven't a chance."

To emphasise his point, he took me out in his own twin-engined rubber-hulled, catamaran to have a look at the gorge itself. Until the lake narrowed sharply to enter the Cabora Bassa gorge, the countryside looked rough but passable. Then suddenly, we were rushing between high and very steep cliffs and I began to see what

Judd meant. In most places the cliffs came right down to the waters edge and looking up, I had a feeling that I could never make it along the top, even allowing for there being water up there.

To make matters worse, the main channel branched off into numerous crossroads that would mean very long detours and I felt my heart sink into my boots.

"There is probably a track or small road that will take you directly into Tete from the start of the gorge," Judd attempted to lighten my gloom. "But it will take you well away from the Zambezi."

Which was not the point of the exercise. I was walking the river and didn't want to travel far inland and away from it.

"Perhaps this Mawaya character will know a way through?" I asked plaintively and Judd smiled.

"If anyone can get you through, he is definitely your man. He has wandered this area for years and knows most of it like the back of his hand. You will like him too. He really is a fascinating character."

I didn't sleep well that night. Images of the terrible terrain that awaited me filled my head and I wondered what to do. I was very fit, but my age was beginning to tell and I was desperately tired. My body ached even more than usual and the prospect of dragging myself through that dreadful gorge filled me with fear. It looked like a recipe for almost certain death.

There was one intriguing aspect to that morning trip in Judd's boat though. As we roared up the gorge and flashed across the many crossroads, Judd and I discussed what would happen if the dam wall further upstream at Kariba burst – something that doom mongers have been warning about for years. My own opinion had always been that in such an eventuality, the sheer weight of water that would hurtle down the Zambezi would be too much for the wall at Cabora Bassa, but Judd didn't agree.

"Most of those side channels are many kilometres long," He told me soberly. "I feel that they would absorb a great deal of the main mass of water, so that although it would be badly battered, the wall itself would survive."

He had a point too, although it wasn't encouraging from my point of view. The prospect of walking vast distances out of my way to circumvent side channels was a horrible one and we had only seen one dugout canoe in the gorge, so there would be little hope of getting a lift across them. I knew that I had a great deal to think about if my walk was not to go the same way as David Livingstone's grand plan to open up the African interior a century and a half previously. I had been fearful of the gorge below the dam wall, but above it was equally frightening and difficult, if not more so. Somehow I had to get through this desperate bit of countryside and reach the relative safety of Tete.

It certainly wasn't going to be easy and I found myself praying that the mysterious Mawaya would come up with a plan that would keep my Zambezi adventure on track.

CHAPTER NINE
(In the Footsteps of Livingstone)

It must have been about noon when I stumbled into Mawaya Hougaard's idyllic little camp on the edge of the lake. Two men rose from a shady veranda to greet me and I approached with some hesitation.

"I am looking for a chap known locally as Mawaya," I announced and one of the men laughed aloud through a bushy black beard. His hair was wild and uncombed but his teeth flashed white through the mass of hair as he announced himself.

"I am the one. The people call me that because they reckon I am a bit of a crackpot. I suppose I am really but don't be alarmed. I am quite harmless."

The other man was Johan's brother Chris, an altogether more serious businessman from Harare who introduced himself and looked me over closely.

"We have heard about you"' He said quietly. "When I heard that an elderly mzungu was walking the Zambezi, I looked you up on the Internet. You are quite a celebrity and I heard in Zim that you are an elephant man."

That made me smile – not the celebrity part, but elephants are very special to me and I am inclined to be fanatical about protecting them as a species. It was pleasing to know that people remembered.

Johan broke enthusiastically into the conversation.

"I love elephants too but I am a tiny voice that will have no influence. People like you can do a lot of good though. Now tell us about your walk and how we can help."

I spent the next half hour telling them all about it before asking Johan the all-important question.

"Is there any way through the gorge or around it without straying too far from the course of the river?"

"Yes," he said and I felt an immediate lift to my spirits, "there is an old trail that goes around the back of Mount Stephanie. The last white folk to use it were David Livingstone and his party, way back in 1863.

'I have only read and heard about it, I'm afraid. I am not even sure where it starts except that it is not far from the entrance to the gorge. I have always wanted to walk it though. Have you got room for a companion?"

I didn't hesitate. I have always travelled alone and at my own speed, but Johan seemed such an open, obliging chap that I reckoned he would prove good company. Besides, he could see me through the gorge which was the point of the exercise.

"I don't walk very fast." I warned, but he waved my objection away.

"I don't suppose we will be able to walk fast," He laughed again – a great big belly laugh that was infectious. "I have a mate in Harare who is an expert in Livingstone's travels, so he will be able to tell us exactly where to go. He will probably want to come with us though."

Having two companions wouldn't be much different from having one I supposed, although it would provide yet another witness to my moments of fright or despair. I might have had the reputation of a fearless adventurer, nut I knew only too well how adversity could get me down and what an emotional weakling I could be.

So everything was quickly arranged. Johan and Chris were off to Tete that evening, but before they left, maps were produced and the pair of them discussed the best places for me to be resupplied once I was past Tete. It was something that had worried me about the Mozambican part of my walk because I no longer had the wonderful Cowbell team supporting my endeavours. I had to carry enough food to keep me going and that pack of mine seemed to be getting heavier by the day.

"We can bring stuff into you by boat or vehicle," Mawaya waved my doubts aside. "If you make a list of what you need, Chris or Francie can buy the stuff in Harare and it will be waiting for us when we reach Tete in ten days or so."

In truth, my only pressing need was for pipe tobacco, but it was fun thinking through what I might need in perfect circumstances and over the next two days, I compiled a list that I left with Mawaya's lady, Francie.

It was short for Francesca, she told me. She was Portuguese and had known and loved Johan for nearly ten years. She showed me to a small, thatched rondavel with *en suite* facilities and told me to make myself comfortable.

"Relax and enjoy yourself," Francie advised. "Take anything you want or need from the pantry and if you require tea, coffee or a cool drink, call one of the staff."

She promised to let me know when dinner was ready and I spent my afternoon exploring a truly lovely camp. Tall shady trees towered over manicured lawns and in one spot, a gigantic stone tree trunk provided an awesome garden feature. I had seen many examples of petrified wood during my wanderings, but this one was a massive trunk that looked to have been cut into slices. How it had been done I couldn't imagine, but it was surely unique and I ran my hands respectfully over the smooth surfaces of the obelisk.

As for myself, I seemed to have landed with my bum in the butter yet again and couldn't help marvelling at how kind and generous the kapenta folk of Cabora Bassa were being to me. Like the black Zambians who had gone out of their way to assist where they could, these white Mozambicans – most of them had actually come from Zimbabwe – were keenly interested in my venture and were only too keen to be a part of it. Although I have always been a loner by nature, I knew that I could not have managed to walk so far without the support of the folk I encountered along the way.

It seemed that ever since meeting Barry Van der Maas at Casindira, I had been pampered and cosseted by amazing people and now it seemed that my journey was taking another new and unexpected turn.

The following evening, Mawaya barrelled back into camp, accompanied by a short, fair-haired man who he introduced as Ronnie Henwood, his historian friend from Harare. On receiving the invitation to accompany us down the 'Livingstone Trail,' Ronnie had wasted no time in driving nearly three hundred and fifty kilometres to Tete, where he met up with Mawaya. The two of them sat me down, beer was produced and they started making plans for our forthcoming safari. For forty minutes, we pored over aerial photographs on Google Earth and even I was able to make out a faint white line through huge hills that they assured me was the path we wanted. I was unconvinced, but for the moment had become a bystander in my own adventure, so was content to let them get on with things.

Two of Mawaya's staff, Moffat Barnabas and Isiah Tito were press ganged into accompanying us, mainly so that they could carry the heavy stuff and make cooking fires when they were needed. They were two cheerful young men and although Isiah's English was very basic, Moffat was another Zimbabwean and supplied a sunny nature, beaming smile and an ability to rustle up tea in the most unlikely stopping places. He also spoke excellent English and these two chaps were to have an immense bearing on the rest of my walk.

Judd Havnar had been called in to supply the boat that would drop us off where the path began and he would also liaise with us along the Zambezi below the dam wall. He would meet us at one of Johan's camps deep inside the gorge and with everything arranged, we settled down to an evening of gentle and for me, fascinating conversation.

A crackpot he might have been but Johan Mawaya Hougaard was an adventurer in his own right and kept me intrigued by his stories about life in the bush. We were totally different in character but remarkably similar in outlook and I found myself almost looking forward to the walk ahead.

* * *

I wasn't sure what to expect as we stood on the shoreline and posed as a group for Judd to photograph. The lake was wonderfully calm and the ride across the water had been uneventful. All the same, butterflies of anxiety were wriggling in my stomach as I contemplated the immediate future.

I have always been content to travel alone and it meant that I could travel at my own pace and do exactly as I wanted. I could walk twenty kilometres a day or two kilometres a day and take days off if I felt like it. Now I would be subject to the whim of others and although Ronnie's first comment to me had been that he couldn't walk very fast either, all four of my companions were considerably younger than I was.

Deciding to merely go with the flow and enjoy myself, I stood back while Johan and Ronnie discussed the direction we should take. Twenty minutes later, we came across a faint but discernible path through the hills and settled down to follow it. Moffat and Johan moved on in front, Ronnie followed them, I came next and Isiah brought up the rear. I was happy with that arrangement and we kept to it over the following days. Johan carried a small rucksack, slung over one shoulder, Ronnie wore a specially adapted green waistcoat that seemed to contain all his kit in voluminous pockets, my pack was considerably lighter than usual, while Moffat and Isiah bore home-made packs, held together with twine. Each of them also carried cooking pots in their hands. We had plenty of water between us and the general atmosphere was one of cheery excitement as we walked Eastward.

It was my fifty-eighth day on the road, so I was pretty fit, but it was difficult to keep Johan from setting far too fast a pace. Both Ronnie and I did our best to rein him in, but the boundless energy of the man kept him pushing ahead and eventually, we just let him get on with things.

Mount Stephanie was named by David Livingstone after a Portuguese queen of the time and my companions were determined to climb it the following day. A huge, brooding hill, it loomed ever closer and after my first look at it, I assured them both that I would wait for them on level ground. The views from the summit were undoubtedly spectacular, but I didn't think my tormented muscles could take that sort of punishment.

That evening, we stayed in Shingira Village where a schoolteacher called Selso took us under his wing. His English was good and although we wanted to camp in the bush, he begged us not to as he was afraid we would be attacked and killed by Renamo bandits.

Renamo (the acronym for Resistência Nacional Moçambicana) were the anti-government movement, responsible for the brutal civil war that had ravaged Mozambique for decades. Originally set up by the Rhodesian Central Intelligence Organisation, they had later been financed and supplied by South Africa and although the war had ended in nineteen ninety-two, their reputation still seemed to worry many Mozambicans. I had repeatedly been warned about anti-personnel mines along the way, but early on had decided that if I kept to paths and avoided bundu bashing, I would probably be fairly safe. After all, most of the paths were used regularly by villagers, so the mines must have long since been lifted or gone off.

Anti-personnel mines last for years in the worst of conditions, but although perhaps wildly optimistic, my reasoning convinced me and after a while, I didn't even think about such things. Mind you, that evening Ronnie found three very old AK47 cartridge cases in the sand, so Shingira had doubtless seen Renamo action in the past.

For Selso's sake, we set up camp in the village itself. Johan lorded it in his little tent, while Ronnie and I slept in the open. It was bitterly cold, but Moffat and Isiah had made a big fire and I kept getting up during the night to keep the flames going.

Oh the bliss of having tea brought to me while I was still wrapped in my blanket! This was definitely adventuring with a difference and made an excellent start to our second day on what we had christened The Livingstone Trail.

The path itself was deeply defined in places, so it had obviously been used for a long time, yet the few people we met along the way seemed terrified by our pale faces. On two occasions, adult villagers fled shrieking at our approach and had to be cajoled back by Isiah calling them in their own tongue. Even with his gentle coaxing, they remained nervous and apprehensive. It made me wonder what they had suffered at the hands of presumably white strangers in the past.

The hills around us were steep and very rocky with gaunt crags and cliffs liberally scattered around their faces. Looking up at them, I couldn't help imagining what events they had witnessed through the centuries. Once upon a time, elephants, lions and other animals would have roamed these valleys, coexisting with the local inhabitants, but all vestiges of wild life had long since disappeared to be replaced by donkeys, chickens and skinny village curs. I couldn't help feeling sad at the way African life has changed under the guise of progress.

Mind you, in this part of the world, I didn't think there had been much progress over the years. The people wore clothes, but for the most part, these were torn and dirty. Their huts were very basic and there were few signs of crops being grown around the villages. Although we were less than twenty kilometres from a giant, modern dam wall, we might as well have been walking through the Africa of long long ago. My ever romantic nature enjoyed that.

We breakfasted on tea and fruit while the village elders solemnly gathered to gaze at us. They must have wondered what sort of world we came from and many admiring glances were directed at Mawaya's tent and my Courtney boots. Ronnie also attracted admiration for his green waistcoat and although we should probably have felt self-conscious about the attention we were receiving, it was all rather fun.

Johan himself was in his element and held Court among the villagers, regaling them with tales of this mad mzungu who was walking right across Africa as David Livingstone had walked a hundred and fifty years previously. He called me the elephants' friend and I felt vaguely embarrassed at the admiring looks directed my way. He meant well though and promised to fly out and drop footballs into the village from his microlight aircraft as soon as he returned home. He had shown me some of the footballs he had had painted before we left Cabora Bassa. They were ornately inscribed with drawings of elephants and messages from both the elephants and myself. His intention was to drop them into all the remote villages of the area and it was a scheme that I thought could prove very successful, so I tried to appear nonchalant about all the praise being directed at me.

We were joined by the local chief, whose name was Luciano, and we started out from Shingira when the sun was high in the sky. Although my pack was being carried for me by a young man called Santos, I struggled to keep up with the small army of men who were to accompany us to Mount Stephanie and show my companions the best way to reach the summit. They didn't call the mountain Stephanie however, the local name being Shipiri Ziwa, which sounded much more romantic.

I was beginning to feel somewhat light-headed by mid-morning and put it down to the extreme heat and the pace at which we were travelling. Then disaster struck and even though I carried only my walking pole, I stumbled as we negotiated a steep rocky path. My knees gave way and down I went, cannoning off Mawaya who also went sprawling and I ended up at the foot of the slope in a bleeding, battered heap.

Isiah leaped forward to pick me up and for a few minutes I was grateful for his strong arms supporting me. The others all rushed to my aid and I waved their anxious queries as to my health away. My legs were shaky and I felt slightly sick, but it passed and as soon as I was able, we resumed the march at a slightly – but only slightly – slower pace. Both Johan and Ronnie kept glancing around at me with obvious concern, but I forced myself on until we reached Dziwa Village.

Word had obviously gone ahead and we were met by a group of ululating women. Wooden chairs were produced and I was grateful to sit down, but Selso who had appointed himself our chief guide told me that I was to play a leading role in a ceremony to propitiate the Spirits of the mountain.

"But I am not going up there," I protested. "Only these two are daft enough to climb it in this heat."

However, Mawaya's early morning speeches had elevated me to almost God-like status among the villagers and I eventually allowed myself to be introduced to the village witch doctor. She was a wrinkled old lady, clad in what appeared to be a tattered blanket and wearing a shiny metal comb in her hair. She rubbed some sort of medicinal paste on to the still raw grazes on my arms and legs and then led me to a solitary Msasa tree, singing loud incantations as she did so.

At the foot of the tree, there was a small hole, filled with something unspeakable and I was given a calabash of liquid and directed to pour a little of it into the hole. I am African enough to have a sneaking respect for tribal spiritual beliefs, so offered my own prayer to whoever was 'up there' as I followed my instructions.

I then had to drink some of the liquid in the calabash and it was not a taste that would prove popular in the fleshpots of the modern world. Pungent and sour tasting, it was obviously a fermented brew and I took a healthy gulp, wondering what it would do to my insides.

The gourd was then passed on for tasting by Johan, Ronnie, Moffat and Isiah, all of whom sipped without obvious relish.

The propitiation ceremony concluded, we resumed the walk, but I was still very shaky and when we came to the shady bed of a dry stream, I was made comfortable on the sand, while Isiah made me a cup of blessedly sweet tea and the others prepared for their mountaineering jaunt. Johan offered to leave someone with me, but I was happy to be alone and told them to go off and enjoy themselves.

"It should take us about five hours, I reckon." Ronnie told me and I waved them away. I was comfortable and in the shade, so looked forward to a restful day to sort out my physical woes.

My Kindle had 'died' on the previous day and after a few more futile attempts to get it going, I gave up and fell asleep on the sand.

Two hours later, my companions were back, having been foiled in their endeavour by the crippling heat.

"There was absolutely no shade up there," Ronnie said after enquiring as to how I felt. "We will camp here for the night and leave Stephanie for another occasion."

They had arranged for porters to help us the following day and at first light, the porters gathered, with Santos proudly claiming his right to carry my pack. Again the pace was much too quick for me, but Johan had the bit between his teeth and pressed on ahead till eventually Ronnie called him back. He too was struggling to keep up with the irrepressible energy of the big fellow.

Mawaya looked suitably abashed at being told off by Ronnie, but his eyes twinkled behind the wild thatch of hair on his face. When I had asked him about the long hair and beard, he grinningly told me that he had vowed not to shave or cut his hair till Robert Mugabe was dead.

"Huh!" I told him. "By that time, you will have disappeared behind it all. That old goat will live for ever."

I was feeling considerably better than I had immediately after my fall though and really enjoyed the magnificent and largely deserted countryside we walked through. This was Africa in the raw and it excited my vaguely adventurous soul. Whether David Livingstone's party really had been the last white people to use this path, didn't matter. I felt a deep sense of privilege at using it myself and the sheer vastness of the terrain soothed my senses. This was surely what my Zambezi Walk was all about.

CHAPTER TEN
(Disaster)

It was one of those idyllic spots that are rare in the harsh panorama of the African bush. Although the mighty hills and rock faces still scowled down at us, we found ourselves in a tiny valley, so green and verdant that it took my breath away.

The valley was fed by two small streams and although my agricultural expertise is nil, even I could see that the soil was rich and loamy. We set up camp in a grove of huge old mango trees, but all around us were bananas, massawa fruit, Cashew trees, cassava and maize plants. They seemed to be growing in a higgledy piggledy jumble, but someone must surely have planted them at some stage. For all that, nowhere could we find the remains of a house, or any building at all for that matter. A couple of scared looking locals passed our grove and we called them over, but even with careful prompting, neither of them could recall ever seeing a white person in this valley. My initial theory had been that it was part of a farm, abandoned after independence, but the farmer and his staff would have had to live somewhere so that didn't hold water.

"David Livingstone mentions this place in one of his journals," Ronnie informed us. "At least he describes a valley that was much as this is, even to the point of having two streams flowing through it."

Strangely, our porters left us when we came into the valley. Isiah said that they were scared of venturing out of their own area in case they were not welcome in another place. It seemed that legacies of the civil war still existed, even in this little piece of Paradise.

There were snakes among the mango trees and during the afternoon, a long green boomslang dropped through the branches to land with a thump beside the spot where Ronnie was dozing. These are slender, arboreal snakes and highly venomous, but they are naturally shy and seldom seen. This chap must have slipped from a branch and was undoubtedly far more upset and frightened by his fall than any of us. Ronnie yelped and leaped to his feet while Johan and I were convulsed with laughter. After a momentary pause to clear its head, the boomslang made off very speedily and we all relaxed once more.

Snakes are a minor passion of mine and although I respect them all, I have never been frightened of them. All snakes will avoid mankind where possible and despite there being millions in Africa, they are rarely seen, unless of course one looks for them. I had seen few along the Zambezi, so the boomslang was a special treat.

Ronnie was not so keen though.

"That was a bloody monster," Was his comment. "The damned thing nearly landed on me."

He was particularly careful making up his bed that evening.

We spent the rest of the day resting up from our exertions and it was pleasant to sit around a fire that evening and wonder who else had seen that enchanted little valley.

Ronnie asked me what I knew about the history of the Zambezi, but apart from it being known as the gateway into Africa and possibly the way to Ophir, the legendary treasure city of Solomon and Sheba, my knowledge was nil. My new friend proceeded to enlighten me.

"It wasn't always known as the Zambezi," Enthusiasm for his subject was readily apparent. "In fact nobody knows when or how that name arrived. In India it has been known about for centuries and they always called the river Oris, presumably after one of their Gods."

"Wasn't there a God called Osiris?" I asked, but I didn't really know what I was talking about and he waved my interruption aside.

"The river between the sea and this gorge was always known locally as Cuwama or Zivama," He went on. 'From Tete to Kariwa was Mpondo or Batondo. Here in the Tete area itself, it was Inyungwi and further west of Kariba gorge it was Nkweni.

'The Victoria Falls was there long before Livingstone named it after his queen and the locals knew it as Chiyongwe or Sheyongwe which basically translates as 'place of rainbows.

'The Arabs used the river as a highway for the transportation of gold, ivory and slaves, looted from the interior and they teamed up with the Bantu in order to decimate the lesser tribal groups and keep the slave trade going.

'The Chinese originally used the river to import their china wares and in the seventh and eighth centuries there was a roaring trade in giraffes that were sent to China.

'It seems weird in this modern day and age," Ronnie mused, his face lit by the flickering flames of the fire, "but the Yanks and the Brits always seem to take the blame for slavery. That idiot Tony Blair even made a public apology to black people for Britain's role in the trade, yet they were merely the end users. The Arabs and Bantu were the suppliers, but that seems to have been forgotten. In fact, it was the British and Americans who brought the trade to an end in eighteen seventy-three, a lot of that due to Livingstone himself."

It was all fascinating stuff and interesting to hear, but to me the river in question will always be the Mighty Zambezi.

We went on at a slower pace the next morning. We had our packs to carry and I was relieved that even Johan seemed to have abandoned his urge to get somewhere as soon as possible. He wandered along, chewing Massawa berries – little yellow jobs that tasted sweet and were, so he repeatedly told us, extremely nourishing.

"That is why the local people don't get sick," He pronounced through a mouthful of yellow juice. "If they do, they just munch on these things."

It was a nice theory and the berries were refreshing, so we humoured him and ate a few ourselves.

Towards noon, we came across a shabby little village where the Headman brought chairs for us to sit on and questioned us as to our journey. He was quite friendly, but the village itself was unprepossessing and dirty, although an incongruous note was provided by a solar panel in the roof of one hut. It turned out to be the local banca, so we had it opened up and bought biscuits and cool drinks for everyone.

Somebody turned on a radio and loud African music blared through the silence, causing Johan to burst into a dance. Two children danced with him and it was a delightful moment in a desolate spot. I was beginning to enjoy my exuberant companion and was glad to have him along. He certainly made life interesting.

Ronnie too was proving himself an easy person to get along with. Although much quieter than the high spirited Mawaya, he had a keen eye for the world around him and we talked a great deal as we wandered on. He told me that he wanted to write a book about Livingstone's travels and I assured him that I would help him wherever possible.

"I will hold you to that." He smiled, but sadly the book was never to be.

It was wonderful to sleep beneath the stars in that massive environment and for once my sleep was deep and refreshing. I awoke in the mornings feeling good and ready for whatever the day would bring and it was always a joy to start off again in the cool early morning air, my four companions looking bright eyed and cheerful around me.

After my fall, Isiah seemed to have appointed himself my personal protector and whenever I felt myself flagging or stumbled on rough ground, a hand would be under my elbow to keep me going. We couldn't really converse much, but his was a comforting presence.

Moffat stayed beside Johan whenever he could and his smile never seemed to waver, even when the Hairy One was on one of his exploratory charges. Ronnie and I no longer tried to keep up with them and we plodded along at our own pace, chatting quietly and both of us aware of the silent but ever watchful Isiah right behind us.

It had been a long day and we had covered a good many kilometres, when we came out on top of a high ridge to see a river on the plain far below. It wasn't the Zambezi, but the Kapoche River, a small tributary. As we looked down on it, we could see Johan and Moffat on the other side of the river. They were tiny, ant-like figures from that distance, but they had a deep grove of large trees just ahead of them and I prayed they would stop and make camp. Instead of which they skirted the trees and were soon lost to sight. I groaned aloud and turned to Ronnie to complain but he was smiling.

"The camp is a couple of kays further on," He said soothingly. "It is easy walking so we will be there well before nightfall.

'We will have to wade across the Kapoche though and it is deep in places, but shouldn't come above our waists. Mind your footing though. This one has a very rocky bed and the rocks are slippery."

Mawaya and Moffat were nowhere to be seen, but I promised to be careful as we approached the water. Before we could attempt the crossing, we were approached by a local villager, who wordlessly handed us a mug of cold water each as well as a roasted mealie cob. It was a touching gesture and we all thanked him, although only Isiah could make himself properly understood.

I was very weary at this stage and had fallen twice during the day so was not happy with my lot. There was no choice but to push myself on though and suddenly, we were walking among giant baobabs. Ronnie kept me going by pointing out places, pertinent to his research into Livingstone's travels. There were spots where the party had camped and another place where one of their number had fallen sick and had to be abandoned for a few days while the rest of them went on.

"It was undoubtedly malaria," Ronnie told me, "but he caught up with them once he had recovered."

I felt sorry for the man involved, but was told that he had been left with food, water and quinine to keep him going. I couldn't help wondering how he had felt to see his friends leaving though and hoped it would never happen to me. I was probably tempting fate, but almost without noticing it, the forest had thinned out and suddenly, I saw a large green tent under a massively thick baobab that had a door built into its side. Johan appeared with a huge grin on his face and I irritably chided him for leaving us behind.

"I knew you would get here today," He boomed. "We can rest up for a couple of days before heading downstream. I have already contacted Judd and he will join us tomorrow if he can get up the rapids."

The camp was in another wonderful spot and overlooked the Zambezi which rolled placidly past us, gleaming like pewter in the evening sunshine. I took my boots off with a sigh of relief, although both my companions warned me not to walk around in bare feet.

"Too many nasties in the sand here," said Mawaya and I promised to wear my sandals at all times.

The following morning Judd came through on Johan's cell phone to say that the boat had broken down but he would meet us further downstream three days hence. Mawaya was grimly disappointed as he had been looking forward to some fishing, but I was relieved to have a whole day of doing nothing.

Like most of its kind, the giant baobab had a hollow trunk and this Mawaya had converted into a pantry. Shelves had been put up inside and the 'room' was secured with a padlocked door. Inside, there were tinned foods of all descriptions and for two days, we ate really well. I wondered that a flimsy padlock could be protection enough in lawless Africa, but he laughingly told me that few people even knew of this spot and those that did, avoided it.

"You won't see a soul here," He promised. "The blokes tell me that it is protected by the local witch doctor so everything we leave behind is quite safe."

Johan went off fishing from the shore the next morning while Ronnie and I went for a walk in the surrounding bush. He was overjoyed when we came to a small river flowing into the Zambezi and found a section of rapids, plunging down the rocks. There were two distinct waterfalls there and he pointed this out with enthusiasm.

"Livingstone describes this as a double rapid," He told me. "This is the first time I have seen it with the water high though. On past visits the water has been lower and I have only seen one, so this is really great. It confirms so much."

It was even greater for me to take a long bath in the Zambezi. We bathed together off a wide, sloping sandbank, both of us keeping a wary eye out for crocs, but it was such a relief to get the dirt and sweat of six days of hard walking off my body.

It was another enjoyably relaxing evening and we swopped stories about Africa and life in the bush till way past my usual bed time. The camp had once been temporary home to Livingstone and his party, inasmuch as they had camped beneath the same baobab. They had doubtless enjoyed a similar fire to sit around and it felt very strange to be sitting in the same place a hundred and fifty odd years later. The wood used in our fire – and presumably in theirs all those decades ago – was from the Sitimbe tree, a type of Leadwood that was abundant throughout the gorge. I had always thought that no wood could match that of the Mopani which burns for ages and gives off a wonderful fragrance, but this was possibly even better. The wood burned slowly throughout the night and to get it going in the mornings required but a couple of gentle puffs before a flame would spring into life.

"Mix the ash with water and it will give you an excellent toothpaste," Said Johan and I promised to remember this if ever I ran out of the real thing.

We were two days ahead of the schedule we had given ourselves, but Johan was anxious to meet up with Judd and do some fishing, so the following morning he and Moffat pushed on while the three of us followed at a more leisurely pace. It felt wonderful to be beside the Zambezi again. Over the two hundred and forty odd days that I had been walking the river, I had grown attached to it and somehow it felt like home. I had seen the Zambezi in all its moods and all sorts of weather. I had seen it as a tiny spring and then a trickling stream. I had watched it hurling itself viciously through gorges or throwing itself over rock faces like a roaring harridan. I had observed it sneaking over wide flood plains and I had watched it purring majestically along like a matronly mother of Africa. I had loved being beside it despite all the challenges it had faced me with. I had enjoyed walking among its people and the few wild animals that still prowled those mighty banks. It had been cruel to me at times and at other times, had soothed me with its majestic benevolence. Truly this was a magnificent watercourse and I knew that I was privileged to have been allowed into its bosom.

But the Zambezi weather was not kind to us when we set off the next morning. A cold, blustery wind blew directly into our faces and with it came speckles of icy rain. My teeth chattered uncomfortably and at times I found it difficult to stay upright when traversing rough ground. Isiah noticed my difficulties and moved up close to me, but even he couldn't help when I fell.

I don't know how it happened, but suddenly I was going down and there was nothing I could do to prevent it. I dropped my walking pole and instinctively put my hand up to cushion my fall, but even so, the weight of my pack drove me face first into the rocky ground. After the first part of my Zambezi Walk, I had gone to see my dentist, Sue Browse in Cheltenham and asked her if she could save my front teeth which were clattering uncontrollably as a result of malnutrition, scurvy and malaria. After a short examination with one finger, her answer had been succinct.

"No."

The five offending teeth had been replaced with expensive plastic ones, but when I fell on this occasion, my immediate thought was that I was glad the proper teeth had gone. Had they not, they would have been smashed out against a rock, which mangled my mouth, but merely pushed the denture plate back into my throat.

Isiah and Ronnie helped me to my feet and we rested for twenty minutes while the latter tried to wash the blood and dirt off my face. I was shaken, but I didn't think any real damage had been done and soon we were on the road again.

At one stage, we came across a family digging for gold and stopped to talk with them. They were making a terrible mess of the countryside with their holes, tunnels and piles of earth, but it was the only money making venture available to them, so I sympathised with their plight.

Mathew told me that he worked the diggings with his two wives and nine children, so it was very much a family business. They managed to extract about a gram per day from the earth, so money was short and they had to keep going. According to my very rough calculations, that was fractionally over an ounce per month. I didn't know what the price for raw gold was, but didn't think that an ounce worth could possibly feed a family of twelve over that time. Much as I disliked what Mathew and his clan were doing to the banks of the Zambezi, I felt desperately sorry for them as we moved on.

There were other families carrying out similar operations and I wondered how long the area could take the strain of all the digging. The gold was obviously there, but if Mathew's amounts were to be taken at face value, it was only there in miniscule quantities. Once again, Mankind was causing huge damage to a beautiful environment.

It was a long day and the chilly weather exacerbated the aching of my face as I stumbled along. Ronnie kept glancing anxiously in my direction and I could see that he was concerned for me, but I waved him on. Half way through the afternoon, we came to a little bay, where Johan and Judd were ensconced on easy chairs and had obviously enjoyed a good day as Moffat was busy cleaning a couple of good-sized tiger fish.

"What happened to your face?" Was the ebullient Mawaya's first question. "Have you been snogging trees again? Perhaps we should fix you up with a local lady instead."

I told him what he could do and settled down thankfully on soft sand. The bay was just below what looked to me a frightening rapid, but Johan assured me that it was quite possible to climb it in a boat. I must have looked doubtful as he promised to take me up that evening.

In the meantime though, I had developed a bad headache, which I put down to banging my face earlier in the day. I was also shivering badly, but it had been a cold and somewhat wet day, so I merely huddled closer to the fire. I have a horror of pills, but took a couple of pain killers with some icy cold coke and felt vaguely better for a while. It didn't last though and although I did go up the rapid with Judd and Johan later on, I struggled to get down a delicious fish supper and went to bed early, even for me. I slept only fitfully and at first light joined the others for tea around the fire. Arrangements were being made for the day ahead and Johan explained.

"Judd and I are going to do some more fishing," He told me happily. "You and Ronnie go on with the blokes and we will meet you this evening at my other camp. It shouldn't take you more than four hours to reach it."

I was feeling a bit peculiar at this stage and struggled to concentrate on anything, but we duly set off and wandered gently through the bush. I have only hazy memories of the next few hours, but Ronnie later told me that I had fallen a number of times and ended up with Isiah holding me up and my legs just not working.

"We sat you down under a tree," He went on. "You were only semi-conscious and I don't think you knew where you were. I was pretty desperate, so kept Isiah with me and sent Moffat on to find Mawaya. We didn't have a clue where he would be, but somehow

Moffat found him during the afternoon and they came back by boat to find us. By God you were lucky."

I had been lucky and I knew it. Had Moffat not been able to find the fishermen, I might well have died out there, particularly as Ronnie and I had made a very basic mistake in our planning. We had left all our kit except a water bottle each in the boat so that we could walk unencumbered. We hadn't even thought to carry a first aid kit with us – an elementary mistake for two experienced bush men.

But Lemon's Luck had been working overtime again and I have vague memories of being loaded gently on to a mattress in the boat and taken downstream. From there, I was put in the back of a truck with the same mattress and driven ten kilometres or so into Tete, where we went straight to a clinic in the suburbs. I wasn't able to speak coherently but my companions explained it all to a pleasant young Mozambican, Doctor Manuel. He immediately diagnosed dehydration and attached me to a saline drip for four hours. He and a motherly nurse who told me her name was Cecilia paid periodic visits to check on me, but otherwise it was a long and uneventful four hours.

The drip worked to a certain extent as I felt considerably better at the end of that time. I was allowed to go back to Johan's riverside lodge at Benga on the other side of Tete and after a few hours of deep sleep, felt almost human again the next day. We went back to the clinic where it seemed that my rocketing blood pressure of the night before had gone down and I was pronounced almost fit.

"Rest for a few days, drink a lot of fluid and eat well," Was Dr Manuel's advice. "After that, come in and see me again and hopefully you can continue your walk."

With only four hundred kilometres to go, I was going to continue it anyway, but I didn't tell him that. My two companions took me back to the lake and I slept the sleep of the dead in my little rondavel. I woke late and staggered outside to be told that we were having a party that night.

"It is to welcome you back to the world and see you off again on your walk," Johan told me cheerfully. "Ronnie and I thought you were a gonner back there. I have never seen anyone so pale. I told you that you have to drink lots of water, didn't I?"

He had repeatedly and I smiled sheepishly, reiterating the fact that I do not like the taste of water unless it is suitably laced with a good blend from Scotland, but as he walked everywhere holding on to a bottle of water, my protests fell on deaf ears and he merely looked smug. He had suggested that I go back to Harare with Ronnie and see a kidney specialist, but quite apart from the fact that it would cost money that I didn't have, I really didn't feel there was anything wrong with my kidneys.

I still felt weak, but as the Carlisles, Goddards and Judd had been invited to the evening bash, I rather looked forward to it.

I think I was talking to Doug and Margi with a beer in my hand when my wheels fell off and I collapsed in a heap on Mawaya's lawn.

CHAPTER ELEVEN
(Interlude)

Built as it is over a huge coal field, Tete is known as one of the hottest places on earth and the departure lounge at the airport was stifling. I was feeling very groggy and unsure about what was happening to me. I had a vague memory of being held up while having a wee during the night, but apart from that, my memory of events over the previous eighteen hours was blank.

Mawaya and Ronnie had told me all about it when I hauled myself shakily out of bed but since then, everything seemed to have moved at bewildering speed.

"We carried you into bed when you collapsed," Johan sounded quite pleased about it all. "You kept wittering on about having a party, but we fixed up a drip and virtually held you down till you fell asleep."

"We didn't dare leave you alone," Ronnie took up the story. "After Johan and I went off to bed around midnight, Moffat and Isiah sat with you through the rest of the night and while you were sleeping, we started ringing various people in the contacts section of your satellite phone.

'Eventually, we raised your daughter in England and she sprang into action. You will be flying to Joburg this afternoon, courtesy of some businessman in Maputo."

My daughter Deborah is a determined woman and hearing that her father was in a bad way, she had contacted an old friend of hers, Kevin Pitzer in Maputo. She asked him to get me to hospital somewhere. Kevin, who owns very successful businesses in Mozambique had sprung to the rescue. I had been collected by one of his managers, driven into Tete once again and taken to another clinic to be checked over. The doctor, a very pretty young woman examined me thoroughly and decided that I had probably suffered a minor stroke and needed to be checked out in a proper hospital. I told her that I was on my way to Johannesburg and she nodded briskly.

"That is good. They will sort things out there. We don't really

101

have the facilities in Mozambique unless you go to Maputo."

I had no intention of going to Maputo and an hour or so later, found myself sweating nervously in Tete airport while trying to make conversation with the young man who was Kevin Pitzer's representative. The frustrated journalist in me normally ensures that I record the names of people I meet, but in this case, my mind was just too wobbly, so to the two gentleman who assisted me that morning as well as the pretty doctor, you all have my sincere thanks.

I couldn't remember saying farewell to Johan and Ronnie, but they later told me that I had burst into tears and promised them that I would soon be back.

"We didn't believe you," Johan later told me smugly. "I reckoned that you would probably survive, but wouldn't be walking any more."

I think it is my advanced age that causes people to underestimate me.

Kevin had booked my flight with LAM (*Linhas Aéreas de Moçambique*) Airlines, a local company and the flight itself would have been pleasant had I not felt so bad. Walking disconsolately through the corridors of O.R.Tambo Airport in Johannesburg, I felt overwhelmed by the heaving mass of people around me and longed to be back in the bush with the four cheerful companions I had left behind in Mozambique.

I also felt a terrible sense of failure. With only four hundred kilometres of my journey ahead of me, I had been found wanting yet again and that hurt. I had had similar feelings when I dropped out of the walk in Siavonga, but then I had known I would be back to resume it. This time was different. If I had suffered a stroke – even a minor one – there was little likelihood of going back. As I moved slowly and somewhat shakily through the vast airport, I wondered what damage it might have done to me. I went through Immigration and Customs in a daze, then wandered into the meeting area and there was my sister, Suzy Lee waiting for me. She had sent me a text on my arrival advising me to ask for a wheelchair to get me through the airport, but I had been stupidly determined to make it on my own.

She rushed to hug me and I was in tears again. Deep sobs racked my body and Suzy Lee kissed my cheek.

"Come on Brother. We are going straight to see Trishie at her clinic."

Trishie was Doctor Patricia Dorman, long the family doctor and an old friend of mine. She too liked her adventures and although they were different from mine, we had exchanged many a fascinating anecdote over bottles of wine. I felt better at the fact I was seeing her and not going to a big hospital.

On the way through the usual Johannesburg traffic queues, I tried to fill Susan in on what had happened, but I remembered so little about the previous two days that I stumbled and stuttered my way through the story. At last we arrived at the clinic though and my sister insisted on getting a wheelchair for me.

"You look as though you will fall over at any minute, Brother," She said cheerfully. "There is no way that I am picking you up off the pavement."

Johan and Ronnie had wheel chaired me in to the clinic at Tete, so it was my second such ride in forty-eight hours, but I was feeling pretty sick, so acquiesced without fuss. Dr Trish was waiting for us and her greeting was unequivocal.

"You look awful," She said without sympathy, "When are you going to grow up and stop doing so much damage to your body?"

"I see the bedside manner hasn't improved." I murmured and she stooped to kiss me on the forehead.

"Come on, let's take a look at you."

For the next twenty minutes this diminutive lady pushed, pulled, prodded and examined various parts of my anatomy. She took numerous samples and after we had enjoyed a fairly long stay in the crowded waiting room, called Susan and me back to hear her verdict.

"Without the necessary scans, I can't be sure about the stroke scenario, but I feel it is unlikely." I felt a surge of relief. "However David Lemon, you are seriously malnourished, dehydrated and anaemic. I want you to go home, rest and fill yourself up with the tonics I am prescribing for you.

'You have to drink lots of water too as your system has taken a big knock."

On the way home, Susan stopped at a chemist where we bought a large tin of some powder that I had to mix with water and swallow by the gallon. It tasted sweetly revolting, but my sister stood over me while I got it down. Then I was put to bed and struggled to sleep. It was winter and Johannesburg can get very cold, but I shivered my way through the night and wrapped myself in my blanket when I got up the next day.

Copious draughts of tea helped but by mid-morning, my teeth were chattering badly and I knew I had malaria. I have been there a number of times and the symptoms are usually pretty obvious. I told Susan and she immediately telephoned Dr Trish. Back we went to the clinic and this time, I was tested for malaria. The results were returned very quickly.

"You should be dead," My medical friend told me somewhat triumphantly. "Not only do you have *plasmodium uvale,* which is a common strain of malaria, but you have the cerebral variety as well. No wonder you collapsed.

'I wonder why they didn't test you for that in Mozambique." She mused and I forbore from pointing out that she hadn't tested for malaria the previous evening either. That might not have gone down well.

I carried the powerful anti-malarial drug Coartem with me, so once home again, took the necessary dosage and went to bed. Two days later I was beginning to feel distinctly better and the following day I was fine.

Before I left her, Trishie had told me to 'do absolutely nothing for three weeks,' then see her again.

"Then I will tell you whether you can continue this damned silly walk of yours or not."

I smiled fondly at my doctor

"Trish, I love you to bits but you know me better than that. I have a mere four hundred kilometres to go with nearly three thousand behind me. I have to go on or I will regret it for the rest of my life."

"So be it," She said firmly, but there was a smile in her eyes.

"Come and see me anyway before you go."

I promised to do so and settled down to rest, but Johannesburg is not the place for peace and quiet. Susan and her husband, John live in a magnificent thatched house called Lusikisiki (where the wind blows) in an upmarket suburb of Johannesburg. The house has rolling lawns and a lovely ambience, but I was still in a city and there were always people coming in and out. On a whim, I rang Inter Air, the friendly domestic airline who had brought me back from Ndola at the end of Part One of the walk. Would they give me a free return flight to Ndola so that I could recuperate properly?

I had written a number of articles about my walk for their In Flight magazine, so they were pleased to oblige and a week after my unceremonious leaving of Mozambique, I was back on lovely Cherry Farm outside Ndola. For two glorious weeks, the 'Brown Ladies,' Shelagh and her daughter, Kaz (short for Katrina) cosseted me, fed me and ensured that I rested. My gaunt appearance eased a bit and I even put on some of the weight I had lost over the weeks of walking. Strength returned to my body and my mind filled with images of paths through the hills, fertile valleys and lovely people in the villages.

Mozambique and the mighty Zambezi were calling me back.

* * *

Three weeks to the day after my somewhat ignominious arrival in Johannesburg, I was back at O.R. Tambo airport, awaiting a Cowbell sponsored flight to Tete. The crowds no longer scared me witless and I felt hugely confident in my ability to walk that final four hundred kilometres. It was actually closer to four hundred and fifty, but in the context of a three thousand kay trek, that didn't seem too daunting.

Mawaya had promised to meet me at Tete, but when I arrived, he was nowhere to be seen. Panicking a little because I had no idea how to reach his lodge or even where said lodge was situated, I went into a car hire company and was making enquiries there when I was clapped on the shoulder by a brawny hand.

"Mr Livingstone I presume," Was Johan's unoriginal comment.

"Welcome back to Tete and the Zambezi."

I was so pleased at seeing him that somehow I managed to break my cell phone and then lost my hat, which he gently pointed out was perched on the back of my head.

"I can see you have all your senses back," He opined gently. "Cool, calm and collected in any circumstances, you are definitely ready for the next step."

But there were to be somewhat dramatic changes to my way of walking, all arranged by Mawaya himself. He announced the changes over supper at his Benga lodge and at first I was aghast.

"Moffat and Isiah will walk with you from now on," He told me. "They are looking forward to the adventure and I have sorted everything out."

"But I can't afford to pay them," I protested. "I can't ask them to walk all that way for nothing. How will they get back in any case?"

"That isn't a problem," There were times when Johan Mawaya Hougaard took my breath away. "They are my employees and will remain on the payroll. In addition, they will have a daily allowance to buy food and whatever you might need along the way. At the end of the journey, I will pay them a nice fat bonus too – provided you make it of course."

"Of course." I muttered, but I was dazed by the generosity of this strange man. I had walked into his camp, a total stranger just a few weeks previously. He had solved my immediate problem of getting through that dreadful gorge, we had enjoyed a few days of great fun in fascinating surroundings, then he and the other three had literally saved my life. Few people recover from cerebral malaria and had I been alone or with less helpful people when I went down with it, I would not be writing these words now. I owed them my life yet here he was, doing his best to make the last part of my Zambezi Walk as easy as possible for me.

"As for how they get back," He went on, "How are you going to get back?"

It was something I had discussed with Andy Taylor in Ndola. The ideal pick up would be by aircraft, but that was an expensive business. First Quantum Minerals had shown interest in the resultant publicity, but if they pulled out, I was in trouble. Andy had promised to drive in himself if he had to, but that really was a last resort. In the event, I had left arrangements to him and tried to put it out of my mind. I brought my attention back to Johan.

"I will even supply you with a tent," He was saying. "Moffat and Isiah will carry it and it will keep the mosquitoes at bay during the night."

Dr Trish had warned me that another bout of malaria would kill me, so much as I dislike sleeping in tents, I knew this was a very necessary addition to my kit and duly expressed my gratitude.

"Why are you doing all this for me Johan?" I asked quietly later in the evening and he bellowed a laugh.

"My Dad always told me that if someone is attempting to do the impossible, I must help him as much as I can.

'You fit the bill My Friend."

I had to be content with that, but in my bed that night, I pondered on the strange mixture of characteristics that held Johan together. Definitely a larger than life character, he was not known as 'Crackpot' for nothing. He had told me that he was a reformed alcoholic, dyslexic, suffered from ADHD which is some sort of attention deficiency complex, had difficulty in staying married and seemingly had more things wrong with him than most people. Yet he was a successful businessman in his own right, had a love of adventure and the wild places as consuming as my own and possessed a heart as big as Africa.

Truly Johan Mawaya Hougaard was a complex character.

To add to my pleasure at being back 'on the road,' Ronnie Henwood arrived from Harare the following day, so the three of us spent a blissful weekend exploring, playing football with local children and generally enjoying ourselves. We visited the magnificent but sadly deteriorating church at Baromo Mission, cruised up and down the river in an open boat and hatched outlandish plans to drift from Kariba to the sea in flat bottomed craft.

"That will be almost as big an adventure as your walk," Johan mused. "We will be at the mercy of the river and only have paddles to get ourselves out of trouble. Wow, I am looking forward to it already."

Ronnie thanked me for motivating him to write his book on Livingstone's travels and promised to keep me closely involved, while Moffat on seeing me for the first time, greeted me with the immortal words, "Ah; the Elephant is back."

Not as memorable perhaps as Stanley greeting Livingstone way back when, but it made me smile.

All too soon the weekend was over and it was time to resume my walk.

PART TWO
(All Change for the Seaside)

CHAPTER TWELVE
(Teamwork on the River)

I had spoken at length to Moffat and Isiah the day before departure and both of them said that they were keen to walk with me and were looking forward to the adventure. Nevertheless, I was nervous as we landed on the Southern bank of the river that Monday morning.

Johan, Ronnie and I had studied maps and Google photographs for hours before deciding that the southern bank offered flatter walking and less populated countryside.

"You should be able to follow tracks and little roads for almost all the way," Ronnie put in thoughtfully. "That has to give you a better chance of success."

Mawaya had provided me with a piece of paper on which he had listed the towns we would pass through with his estimated mileage between them. He had also written in the number of days he estimated it would take us to go between these places and that gave me an incentive to beat his estimates. Thus armed and prepared, I said my farewells on the river bank, shook hands and thanked them both before resolutely turning my back and bidding my new companions to start walking.

Suddenly four hundred – Mawaya's 'chart' reckoned four hundred and fifty – kilometres felt like an awfully long way to walk.

It was my sixty-ninth day on the road, although the sixty-eighth had been some time previously. We walked in single file with Moffat in front, then myself and the ever watchful Isiah (Moffat called him Zaire) bringing up the rear. He obviously hadn't forgotten my falls and ultimate collapse and I could sense his protective presence close behind me.

It took us a long time to get out of Tete. We lost our way in some vegetable gardens and were shouted at by one elderly gentleman tending his crop. Perhaps he thought we wanted to steal his mealies but whatever the case, he reduced my companions to hysterical giggles. Mind you, we did make a quick tactical withdrawal.

Another chap called Andreas stopped to talk and told Moffat that he had seen me and marvelled way back in Zumbu nearly three months previously.

"Do you not remember me Sir?"

I didn't, but assured him that his face was familiar, so we were all happy.

Prior to my breakdown, there had been no real urgency to my walking and I had tried to enjoy myself as much as possible. My attitude had changed with the enforced break and events leading up to it. Suddenly I was in a hurry to get the walk over before anything else went wrong. Trishie's warning about any further bouts of malaria lurked in the back of my mind and I dreaded any other disasters that might crop up. I had to get the whole concept of walking the Zambezi behind me and that meant reaching Chinde as soon as I could.

So I was determined to set a good pace and push the three of us along. Mind you, sitting by the river and watching the sun go down that first day back on the road, the sheer peacefulness of Zambezi evenings made me feel at home again. I knew that once my journey was all over, I would be devastated and would miss the tranquillity of life on the river.

At the same time, I was scared that fate would step in again and prevent me from achieving what had become a major ambition. My attempt to walk the Zambezi had begun as little more than a whim and a longing to get away from the shackles of modern life in the industrial world. Over the months though, this had hardened into determination to finish what I had started. I had been through so much both physically and mentally that if I didn't manage to achieve my goal, I would regret it for the rest of my life.

Besides, I felt that I owed a great deal to so many people who had befriended and supported me along the way. To fail or give up at this late stage, would surely be letting them all down. I just had to reach the sea and thanks to Mawaya Hougaard's helpful generosity, I had an excellent chance of doing so.

Cell phone reception in Zambia had been very spasmodic and determined by proximity to the few masts that seemed somewhat haphazardly placed. Mawaya and Ronnie assured me that I would have no difficulty with reception on the last stage of my journey, so I bought myself a cheap Chinese cell phone in Tete, but soon discovered the reason for its fantastically low price. No matter how often I charged the battery with my Power Monkey, the damned thing would last but a few minutes before flashing the message that it needed recharging. Moffat and Isiah had similar phones, but theirs were fine, so I had just been unlucky in my choice, but I knew that I would have to buy a replacement as soon as possible. There were telephone masts all over this part of Mozambique and I had promised to keep a number of concerned folk informed as to my progress.

Besides, it was always comforting to receive text messages, none more so than the occasional 'Go Madala Go' missives that regularly came in from Alexis the Rasta in Lusaka.

But apart from the regular communications, I was beginning to feel ever more like David Livingstone. Unlike Ronnie Henwood, I was no expert on the Great Man's travels, but from what little I had read about him, he had porters and bearers to carry his kit, trackers to guide him along and camp servants to get his tent up, light the fire and prepare his meals. I had covered nearly two thousand kilometres carrying my own load and doing everything for myself. Now in Moffat and Isiah (I too was starting to call him Zaire) I had my retinue of bearers and camp staff altogether in two sturdy bodies.

They were incredibly different in temperament and skills, but blended together and I think that with me in ultimate charge, we made an excellent team. Moffat at the age of thirty-two combined sound common sense with a cheerful disposition and despite his small but chunky stature was very strong. Isiah was nine years younger and although he told me that he was married with a child, danced and sang his way through life. He loved stopping beside the road when we encountered children and if they were playing football, would join in with cheerful abandon. He used his phone to blast forth music, but I soon grew fed up with the noise and made him wear earphones.

He also loved chatting up the ladies, did young Zaire and both Moffat and I teased him unmercifully. He took it all with a cheerful grin and sometimes I found it difficult to reconcile this shambling young clown with the strong man who had done so much to keep me going just prior to my collapse in the gorge. The one thing that worried me about Zaire's make up was the fact that he had an incredibly loud and high pitched laugh. It was funny and infectious to begin with, but I knew that it would tend to irritate when times were difficult.

And it did, but I hadn't the heart to tell him off.

We soon developed a routine to our walking. I would wake with the first shimmering of daylight and yell for the two of them to get up. While I cleaned my teeth, they would get a fire started and a cup of tea or coffee would be prepared for me before we moved out of camp. With the greatest of respect to Moffat's culinary expertise, it was occasionally difficult to taste the difference between his tea or coffee, but it was made and presented with a big smile that always made it taste better.

The lads slept together in one tent and this would be dismantled and rolled up by Isiah, while Moffat would sort mine out. Once on the road, we walked at a brisk pace for the first couple of hours, then would stop for more tea in mid-morning, before resuming at a gentler speed.

We were passing through heavily occupied country at this stage and would normally camp fairly close to a village. Tents would be erected and a meal prepared which we ate in the early evening. I no longer had to rely on my health gruel either as Mawaya's daily allowance allowed us to buy chickens, fish and fruit from roadside vendors. The chickens would often be intercepted while on their way to market, feet tied to bicycle handlebars and heads dangling. They would not have won any prizes for taste or quality in the western world, but I enjoyed the meals, although I ensured that the fowls were butchered well out of my sight.

We ate plenty of ncima and joy of joys, Moffat varied this with rice as a welcome replacement. Remembering the lessons of scurvy on part one of the walk, I ate my vegetable relish when it was served up and as a treat, Moffat would occasionally prepare what he called 'salad,' which was actually a basic fruit salad. It is amazing how delicious a mixture of banana and paw paw can be on a hot day.

And it was hot – very hot! By ten in the morning the temperature would be up in the high thirties and early afternoons, we all felt as though we were walking through a furnace. Remembering all the advice I had received, I drank a lot of water, although I usually flavoured it with Cowbell Drink o Pop powder – sickeningly sweet, but to my jaded palate, decidedly preferable to the taste of plain water.

We frequently stopped to chat with locals, but soon it was only Zaire who could make himself understood. Even Moffat was out of his depth and we had to rely on the younger man to translate everything. This could be irritating, as on many occasions I felt he was telling me what he thought I wanted to hear.

The one disadvantage to travelling with my two reprobates was that they liked to walk on tracks and roads. Sometimes these took us well away from the river and while I knew we were going in the right direction, I was frustrated at not being beside the Mighty Zambezi. Walking on roads was not the point of my adventure and I fretted whenever we went inland, even though the going was much easier.

Once our camp was set up and the evening meal prepared, Moffat and Isiah would often head for the local village and enjoy an evening out. I tended to retire early to my tent in order to avoid the mosquitoes, although very occasionally I would sit on by the fire and admire the incredible night sky of Africa. Unlike Europe where stars seem to wink on individually, here, the Evening Star (Venus to the experts) would appear as darkness began to build, then as soon as night came down, the sky would be lit up with a vivid panoply of stars and constellations. The Milky Way was almost custardy in its density and the shimmering beacons of the Southern Cross and Orion were soothing to my soul. I watched for shooting stars and satellites, seldom going for more than a minute or two without seeing one or the other. Despite the mosquitoes, star gazing always brought my days to a wonderful end.

So it was that my life on the road developed into a daily routine that – apart from the stars -was almost dull in its sameness.

I had been on the road for two hundred and fifty odd days without sustaining a blister or sore feet but this was about to change. We bought supplies and sweet, fizzy lemon drinks in Dewe Village, where Moffat entered negotiations with a couple of hefty cyclists who agreed to carry our packs for fifty meticais each. Wandering on, I really did feel like David Livingstone, ambling behind my own little wagon train entirely unencumbered. Moffat carried my little pack, while Isiah swung a cooking pot in each hand and I walked freely with only my walking pole. This was the life!

The cyclists had a hefty pack on each machine, but at the next village, one of them dropped out with some form of mechanical problem. Nothing daunted, my two cut throats loaded both packs on to one cycle and Moffat decided that he would ride the ruddy thing. Off he set with a definite wobble but shortly after he disappeared around a bend, we heard the crash and found him sprawled across the road, his legs pinned beneath the bicycle and the packs.

He received little sympathy from me and a great deal of ribbing from Zaire and the other bloke. Eventually, the load was retied and off we set once more. The day was hot and the track we were following was rough and uneven, but I was annoyed when one foot began to hurt. There was no particular reason for this. I had travelled on far rougher paths over the months and with a load on my back. Now I could feel my feet blistering. I stopped by the road to change my socks and could see that the soles of both feet were red and raw looking.

Off we went again but soon I was starting to hobble as walking became ever more uncomfortable. We had a long, high ridge to cross and going down the other side was excruciating, but there was nowhere suitable to camp so I just had to keep going. We weren't moving with any great speed as the overloaded bicycle was difficult to control, but after another hour, I had to call for a rest, something I did not enjoy doing.

My socks came off again and there were white marks under my toes on both feet. I presumed these were embryo blisters and wondered what was happening. My feet were hardened from weeks on the road, Courtney boots were the best in the world and mine were relatively new, while my socks were thick and soft. Why then were my feet suddenly blistering?

Eventually I took my boots off and slipped sandals over my socks. That made life slightly easier and in mid-afternoon we passed through Maranke Village on the edge of the broad Ruenya River. There was little water, but a vast acreage of blindingly white sand lay ahead of us. Half an hour later, I called a halt for the day and we made camp in a small wooded valley. This time I took everything off my feet and kept them in a bowl of deliciously cold water. Having little experience with blisters, I wasn't sure how best to treat them and resolved to walk in sandals, carrying my boots until my feet recovered.

The following day, I had messy white blisters beneath my toes and my walking pace was reduced to a painful hobble, even though my boots were now part of Isiah's load. I still couldn't understand why this disaster had befallen me and my pain during another long, hot morning was as much mental as physical.

Gradually the situation improved, although it was a few days before I was able to walk in boots again. Moffat and Zaire had adjusted their pace to suit my hobble and one morning, the former cheerfully informed me that I was 'walking much better.'

Seven days after they had arrived so unexpectedly, the blisters had reduced themselves to red marks on my skin and were never to trouble me again. To this day though, I have no idea what caused them.

CHAPTER THIRTEEN
(Massengano and Mopani Trees)

I could see what appeared to be walls on the top of a nearby hill. They were visible from a long way off and as we approached, I asked Moffat what they were.

"Fort Massengano," He told me cheerfully. "A favourite place for Mister Ronnie. Do you want to see it?"

After a moment of indecision, I decided that I did, so we branched off the road we were following and made for the hill. Reaching the fort necessitated a fair old climb and although my feet were infinitely better, they still hurt, which accounted for my momentary indecision. It was another hot morning and we were all puffing and panting by the time we reached the fort, but once we did, I decided that the discomfort was definitely worth the effort.

Ronnie had told me about Massengano Fort before I left Tete and had recommended a visit. The place had been built sometime in the seventeenth century and used as a fighting command base for many generations. A metre thick in places. the walls were built from rocks piled on top of each other and although some of them had fallen down or crumbled away, the place was in excellent condition. It was obviously kept clean by local villagers as there was none of the usual rubbish lying about.

"The local people worry about the Spirits that are still left here," Moffat told me and I have to admit that I could sympathise with their worries. The fort had been built around a large baobab tree and it felt deeply spiritual. My companions were obviously as fascinated as I was and the three of us wandered around open mouthed as we explored the site.

It probably covered a hectare of hill top and I could see what were obviously the remains of a guard room and soldiers' quarters. The cannon embrasures were all still intact and through them we had a commanding view of the countryside in all directions. There was a small square that must have been a parade ground in days of yore and I could almost feel what those forgotten soldiers must have felt all those centuries ago. They had been occupying troops in a hostile environment, but from their hilltop eyrie, they would have been well able to fight off all but the most determined attack. I made a mental note to research any battles in the area and having thoroughly explored the place and taken dozens of photographs, we sat quietly and enjoyed the atmosphere.

On one side and far below, we could see the road we had come along and just beyond it, the Zambezi wallowed past in slow and gentle majesty. There were abundant fields on that side, but to the south, all I could see was endless bush with mighty baobabs reaching proudly toward the heavens at regular intervals. Even now, it all looked vaguely hostile although looking down I watched a cyclist wobbling down the road and then a group of youngsters driving three head of cattle toward some unknown market. Their calls drifted up to where I sat and I couldn't help identifying with those Portuguese soldiers of long ago. I too had occupied similar positions, though not as well fortified during the bush war in my own country and I wondered if the soldiers of yesteryear had felt as nervous as I had during their own troubled times. I presumed that many of them would have been conscripts far from their own home, now finding themselves marooned and isolated in this magnificent but to them, totally alien spot.

How would they have felt when sentries spotted the advance of native warriors and how had they reacted to attacks? I didn't know and never would, but I could imagine their feelings of fear and bewilderment at the predicament in which they found themselves.

I would have like to have spent the night in that lonely fort, but Moffat looked scared when I suggested it.

"The villagers would never allow that Boss. They would feel we are disturbing the Spirits."

He was probably correct and a little reluctantly we wandered down the hill and back to the road before heading on. A couple of kilometres further east, we came across what must have been a governor's mansion or perhaps the house occupied by senior military officers in those long gone days. This was in worse shape than the fort itself, but close to it was the remains of a prison, also pretty dilapidated but with heavy bars still in place across the windows. Unlike the actual fort, these ruins had an air of menace about them and I wondered how many miscreants, murderers or mutinous soldiers had been incarcerated, tortured and perhaps executed within its walls.

In fact, the difference between the ruins was very marked. In the fort, the air had been warm and welcoming, whereas the prison was cold and left me feeling clammily uncomfortable. Chiding myself for an over imaginative idiot, I reasoned that the fort had been built on top of a hill so that it was under the direct rays of the sun, whereas the prison was lower down and surrounded by massive trees. Of course, one building was decidedly chillier than the other.

It didn't help though and this time, I was glad to be back on the road.

We had spent almost an entire morning exploring Massengano and I decided to call a halt for the day and enjoy a bath and shave in the river itself. We made camp, the tents were set up and I duly had a wonderful cooling dip in the Zambezi – with one eye open for crocodiles of course.

That evening a motor cycle puttered into camp and a bespectacled young man greeted me with a big smile. He introduced himself as Luciano Juarque and proudly announced that he was the chief of the whole area. With Zaire interpreting, I complimented him on the ruins and he complained that there were few paying visitors to the spot nowadays. Although I was secretly pleased about that, I commiserated with him and we spent a pleasant half hour talking about world affairs. He was obviously well educated and told me that he had been to Portugal, but Massengano was his home and his personal fiefdom.

Moffat took a photograph of us sitting companionably on the grass before the chief puttered away into the evening, leaving me reflecting that it had been an excellent day, despite us not covering many kilometres.

We had other visitors that evening too as a number of local villagers popped in, having had any fears they might have entertained about us banished by Chief Juarque's visit. They were friendly and curious, so Moffat bought us a small rooster for supper and we finished off the day with roast chicken and rice.

I went to bed feeling that I could come to enjoy my leisurely existence.

Our immediate destination at that stage was Tambara Village at the mouth of Lupata Gorge and I felt very pleased with myself when we reached it in five days, rather than the seven which Mawaya had estimated as our travelling time. We camped in a large grove of Massawa trees and for a while I sat on my bedroll with my back against one of the trees. The other two were putting up tents or doing whatever it was that they did in new places and while I was enjoying the sunshine, I felt a movement below my bottom.

Looking down I froze as a large reptilian head emerged from beneath my pack and moved up between my legs. It was a dark brown colour and I moved not a muscle as the snake looked around, flickered its tongue then proceeded to haul itself out from beneath me. Centimetre by centimetre it emerged and I hardly dared breathe as I didn't know what species it was. Any movement was likely to provoke a bite and if it was poisonous, I was a long way from anywhere so would be very ill and might even die.

It felt like an age before the snake was in the open, but once on the grass, it moved leisurely away from me and disappeared into longer grass some ten metres away. It was probably about a metre and a half in length with few markings on a very dark brown body. I felt it was probably a brown house snake and breathed a sigh of relief when it went. I do enjoy snakes, but being that close to them and helpless can be nerve wracking at times.

From where we were camped I could see the mouth of the gorge and although I had been told that it was shorter and not nearly as wild as Cabora Bassa, I asked Moffat whether there was any way around it. We were surrounded by large rolling hills and after making enquiries among the locals, he came back to report that there was a road through the hills that came out at the other end. This was also one that had been used by Livingstone all those years before and a local elder was produced who promised to take us through it the following day.

Quite apart from the brown house snake – if that is what it was – Nyansorro or Lupata as Johan had put it down as on his chart – was an interesting stop. The village itself was called Tambara, but Nyansorro was the local name for the mouth of the gorge. Apparently it meant 'great head' which was doubtless due to a huge rock face at the entrance. The Massawa trees appeared to have been deliberately planted many years previously and now all belonged to one man, who had set himself up in business as a Massawa farmer.

His name was Zachariah Samson and he sat down to talk with me. He told me that he had fifty-three trees in his orchard and he made a decent living from them. He felt that they had grown naturally, but that seemed a little far-fetched to me. We had passed a number of Massawa trees along the road and they seemed to grow everywhere, but this particular collection was too regimented to be anything other than planted by man.

Zacharia's wife and five children were all involved in cropping the fruit from the trees and wherever I looked there were piles of Massawa berries, each pile protected from thieves and predators by a little boma of thorn branches. Some were green, some were yellow and some were the bright orange of ripeness. He told me that although he had customers coming from far afield, most of his crop would be made into beer, for which there were even more customers. With a little grin, he shouted to one of his working children and the tot approached with a bottle of cloudy looking liquid. I was invited to have a slurp so I did and the brew didn't taste bad. I had the feeling that it was probably explosively alcoholic and the drink left a sort of furry feeling on my palate, but I could understand how people could enjoy it.

Although his season only lasted from April to September, Zacharia reckoned to harvest at least a ton of fruit during that time. To actually reap the fruit, it was a question of shaking each individual tree – he gave me a demonstration – so that the berries cascaded on to the ground from where they were collected by the children and sorted into heaps for further ripening. I asked what happened with stubborn berries that refused to fall when shaken and he gave me another demonstration, this time taking his shoes off and shinning up a very straight tree trunk, using his hands and feet to propel him upwards. Despite having young children, Zacharia looked almost as old as me so it was an impressive performance.

The grove of trees was a veritable oasis of peace in what appeared to be a troubled and hostile landscape. Massive rocky hills frowned their disapproval at our intrusion on their domain and I could see the usual rock faces and cliffs scowling down at me. Looking up at those inhospitably huge hills, I prayed that the track we would follow the next day would not mean difficult walking. My feet were much better than they had been, but they still felt vaguely painful and very uncomfortable.

That evening we had a bush fire. It started in long grass that bordered the Massawa plantation and the first I knew of it was a crackling noise that arrived from nowhere shortly before the sun was due to go down. Grey smoke suddenly roiled through our camp and I yelled to Moffat that we had to take a hand and do something.

Quite what I wasn't sure. As the flames came ever closer, we beat them into submission with leafy branches, but the wind was in our favour and I dreaded to think what would happen if it suddenly changed direction. A little to my surprise, Zacharia showed no signs of alarm at the roaring conflagration. He merely shrugged his shoulders and told me that this happened occasionally and that his trees would see it through.

Moffat and I patrolled across the line of the fire, beating out stray flames, but our efforts were hindered by a very drunken gentleman who was determined to have an impassioned conversation with both of us. What he was talking about was not readily apparent to Moffat or myself, but eventually Zacharia managed to usher him gently out of the way.

It took a good forty-five anxious minutes for the fire to die down, apart from occasional small flare ups, but I had a very restless night, not helped by loud squeals of laughter from the tent occupied by my companions. Quite what caused the hilarity I didn't know, but eventually I bellowed a warning into the night and silence descended.

I think at this stage of the walk, Moffat and Isiah were enjoying what they looked upon as an extended holiday with bonuses. Yet for me it was all deadly serious. I needed to finish the walk. I needed to be able to say that I had done it. I also needed to be strong enough both physically and mentally, so sleep and a general sense of tranquillity were very important.

Although I still felt privileged to be free as the breeze, I wasn't enjoying the adventure as much as I ought to have been. The fear of failure, particularly at this late stage was eating away at me and to see the two youngsters really enjoying life and taking it easy whenever possible was making me irritable.

Isiah was loving it though and was never happier than when discussing the walk with villagers, who he would usually collect together and pose for me to photograph them. He made sure that he was in the centre of all such photos and would then spend minutes showing the camera to the villagers, presumably basking in their incredulity at such a modern invention. He also loved to be photographed with young women and when Moffat also started chatting up the ladies, I sourly asked him whether he was after yet another wife.

For me it seemed very stressful, yet looking back on it, I really don't understand why. I was very fit, I was not carrying my normal thirty-kilogram load and virtually everything was being done for me. All I had to do was keep myself relatively tidy and walk.

* * *

Zacharia Samson had volunteered to show us the path through the hills that would take us around Lupata Gorge and although we made a late start, he had brought with him the Elder who Moffat has spoken with the previous day. They both looked pretty ancient, but happily volunteered to carry packs. Once again I walked relatively unencumbered, which was as well because we had some serious climbing to do. The little track wound its way between rocks and in places was achingly steep. The fact that Livingstone and his party had used the same track all that time ago was vaguely interesting but quickly forgotten in the sweaty toil of getting over those hills. Besides, Zacharia assured me that tribal lore had it that the Livingstone party had used donkeys and porters to carry their equipment. My little convoy was not nearly as grand and we sweated our way up a precipitously steep gradient.

Conversation between my companions soon died away and the only sounds to breach the eerie silence of the countryside were the crunch of my Courteney boots on rocks and the laboured breathing from all of us.

Three hours after leaving Nyansorro, we reached the top of a large ridge and Zacharia announced that he and his companion were leaving us and heading home. Indicating the path, we needed to take, he waved aside my offer of payment, so I gave them each a packet of fish hooks. Before leaving Britain for the first leg of my Zambezi Walk, I had bought a few hundred small hooks and divided them into little plastic packets containing ten apiece. Handing these out in lieu of money had proved very successful throughout the journey and Zacharia smiled his thanks and clapped his hands together in gratitude.

So as not too seem too sexist, I had also invested in a number of small packs of assorted needles for ladies who helped and when I added one of these to my 'payment,' the old man positively beamed.

For all that, it was a blow to hoist a pack back on to my shoulders. Isiah was carrying my personal pack and I didn't envy him the job, but I had to carry something and even though my load was lighter, my shoulders and back ached with the strain.

There was nothing for it though. Resting for any length of time was out of the question. We were a long way from water and the day was hot, so we needed to get back to the river as soon as possible. I chivvied my reluctant companions along and promised that we would camp as soon as we had adequate supplies of water.

The going was rocky and the descent was steep, so we were all sweating and weary by the time we reached level ground again and Moffat begged me to stop. Somewhat reluctantly I agreed and we made our way into a grove of large Mopani trees where we lay down in blissful shade. I could feel my muscles relax and wanted to sleep, but we were still very low on water so I knew we had to keep going. After thirty minutes of rest, I pulled Moffat and Isiah to their feet and off we went again.

It was not proving a good day, but at last we found a road that seemed to be going in the right direction and half way through the afternoon, we came across a well- stocked banca with a group of men gathered outside. With a collective sigh of relief, the three of us took off our packs and joined the men. It was a convivial gathering and to my delight, one young chap spoke reasonable English, so we were able to have a conversation.

Elias Mapfumo told me he had spent most of his life in Lusaka, but was now working on a new road that was being built by the Chinese. As we hadn't seen a vehicle in days, I queried the logic behind such a project and he explained with a frown on his face.

"There is a lot of timber being felled in the area and they need the road to get their lorries in and remove the trees. The tree felling and road building provide a lot of employment, but the Chinese are hard task masters. We work long hours and if a man is sick or injured, he loses his job."

I had heard similar tales among road workers building a highway above Sesheke in Zambia and I stifled a sudden feeling of apprehension as to how far Chinese tentacles are stretching into rural Africa. In Zambia, vast swathes of countryside had been devastated by road builders and a huge proportion of the country's timber had been exported or just razed to provide cheap living space for workers, but nobody seemed to be looking to the future. For the Chinese, it was merely a matter of instant profit and I have never liked that sort of thing. I resolved to take a close look at what was going on in Mozambique, but although I didn't know it then, it was going to break my heart.

When I asked Elias where the tree felling – 'timber marketing' he called it somewhat grandly – was taking place, he waved an expansive arm.

"From here to Nyakafura," He said. "Even beyond there – perhaps even to Caaia. They have told us they will take all the trees and the road will benefit our community."

He took us down a narrow, winding path to the Zambezi and it felt wonderful to see that grand old lady ambling past. The tents went up, chicken and rice was prepared and while Moffat was cooking, I examined my legs which were beginning to give me trouble again.

This time it wasn't my feet, which seemed to have fully recovered from their inexplicable failure a week or so previously. As always I was walking in shorts, so my legs were invariably scratched and bleeding. This attracted flies, of which Mozambique seemed to have more than its fair share. They wallowed in my blood and obviously enjoyed the stuff as they always seemed reluctant to move off, even though I flapped continuously at them with a handkerchief.

A couple of my scratches looked red and infected while on the inside of my right calf, what had started out as a tiny hole from a *wag n'bietjie* thorn had expanded to the size of a ten penny piece. This too was looking pretty angry and I applied liberal dollops of antiseptic cream to all the afflicted places.

The main problem as always on my walk was keeping my various cuts and grazes clean. It wasn't too bad when I could bathe in the river, but Moffat and Isiah preferred walking on tracks and roads to ploughing through the bush and this frequently led us far away from the Zambezi. It made water even more precious and I couldn't afford to waste the stuff on keeping my wounds clean. I found it frustrating, but I suppose roads were considerably easier on my exposed arms and legs.

Before I went to bed that evening, I applied more antiseptic and resolved to keep an eye on the round sore.

* * *

The following morning, I had my first look at the tree felling operation and it was even worse than I had feared. After walking past a tented camp with three large flatbed lorries outside, we entered an area of total devastation.

The Mopani tree (*Colophospermum mopane* to the experts) is a truly African tree that only grows in hot, dry, low-lying areas to the north of southern Africa. It has butterfly shaped leaves and thin seed pods, but it forms a vast blanket of forest across the region. It is regularly used as firewood by indigenous people and in Zambia particularly, a tremendous number of trees are cut down and made into charcoal. Government statistics estimate that four hundred thousand hectares of forest are lost every year and that is bad enough, but what I saw on the road to Nyakafura made my blood run cold.

The one attribute that makes Mopani particularly desirable to people like the Chinese is that the tree grows very straight, often to a height of eighteen metres or more. The wood is hard and durable so can be fashioned into almost anything and will last for decades. Wherever I looked, the trees had been cut down to within a few centimetres of the ground, leaving a landscape of ugly stumps that made me want to cry. Massive logs had been left in piles for collection and I started counting individual piles before giving up the exercise as a waste of time. Suffice it to say that the smallest pile I counted contained a dozen tree trunks and the largest in excess of eighty. This was carnage on a grand scale and to my mind was ripping the heart and soul out of Africa.

The workers I spoke to told me that the logs were collected and driven to Beira and Maputo before being shipped to China. Later I was to hear that the majority of them were made into wooden stocks for Kalashnikov assault rifles, but there was no way of verifying that I'm afraid, even in this magical age of the Internet.

We followed the logging road throughout that day and flat-backed transporter lorries, laden with the corpses of murdered trees continually thundered past us in both directions. All three of us were soon caked in yellow dust and probably made a comical sight, but my heart was sore. At one point, I branched off into a yard where logs were stored and started counting again. I had reached around five hundred when a shouted instruction made me lose count. A large man wielding an AK rifle and yelling at us in Portuguese came rushing up and although it was pretty obvious that he was asking who we were and what we were doing there, I couldn't understand a word.

As calmly as I could, I asked in English for whoever was in charge, but he couldn't understand me and Moffat tugged anxiously at my shirt.

"We had better go Boss," He muttered. "This man is very angry and might shoot us with that gun.

'Or he might take us prisoner," He added unhelpfully but I knew he was right.

Bidding the angry man a coldly dignified farewell, I turned on my heels and walked away, Moffat and Isiah close and half running on either side. There was another shout from behind me but I ignored it and walked on. I had avoided a confrontation I suppose, but felt vaguely ashamed of my cowardice.

Looking back on that incident many months later, I know I should have forced a meeting with someone, but at the same time it would not have helped my Zambezi Walk or any of us had we been taken hostage.

As we wandered on, I found myself seething with angry resentment at the wealthy nations of the world and the greed of modern man. I thought bitterly about the words of Joseph Wood Kutch, an American writer and naturalist whose work I had read as a boy. I couldn't remember the exact wording of the piece that came to mind, but it was on the lines that when a man despoils a beautiful work of art, we call him a vandal, but when he despoils a beautiful work of Nature, we call him a developer.

How apt that seemed and it took me a long time to calm down.

Out of things. Ronnie nurses me through cerebral malaria.

Moffat, Myself and Isiah with Johan's dog Whisky.

A fascinating spot - Massengano Fort.

I was setting a cruel pace and my companions were faltering.

Chinese logging lorry in Chema

With Tribal Elder in Mozambique

A novel way of carrying backpacks

Made it! The main street in Chinde.

It is all over. Posing by the sea while Moffat and Isiah frolic in the background.

Posing with Isiah and Moffatt beside the First Quantum aircraft

And with my main sponsor, Andy Taylor of Cowbell.

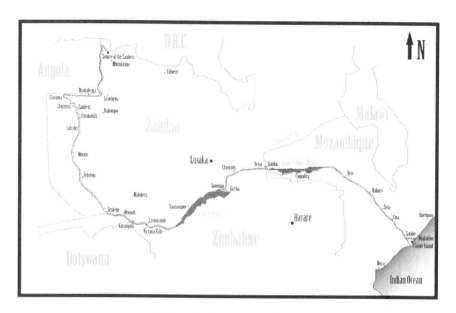

Map of the route taken

CHAPTER FOURTEEN
(A Chieftain's Life)

Tambara Village had been known as Nyansorro, but we reached the genuine Nyansorro Village one hot Sunday afternoon. All of us were sweating copiously and I had the added frustration of being on a road again and probably a goodly distance from the Zambezi.

The village itself was an impressive place, set on both sides of the road and embracing a school, a brick-built shop and a football field. Houses and huts were set back from the road and as we had learned that there was a chief in residence, I asked to see him.

A young man carrying a makeshift football led the way and I entered a small complex of huts around a courtyard where an elderly man sat at a table beneath a large tree. He greeted us politely and through Isiah, I asked him if it would be alright for us to camp in his area.

"Camp here," He invited, indicating an open area beside the courtyard. 'We enjoy having visitors so you will be very welcome."

His name was Tidairana Ajuda Maduapera and he was chief – or *chef* as they call it in Mozambique – of the Nyansorro area through which we had been walking for the past few days. He watched as our tents were set up and half an hour later, the three of us were summoned back to his presence and presented with a meal of fish and ncima. It was too hot to be hungry, but the gesture was a kind one and I couldn't help reflecting that this was the first time that we had been offered food by a Mozambican. I had been fed in other villages, but always by Zimbabweans who are notorious for their hospitality.

Mind you, it was very much Sunday lunch with a difference. The chief and I sat opposite each other while my two reprobates perched to one side. Around us the village livestock consisting of goats, dogs, chickens, pigs and guinea fowl congregated and edged ever closer in hopes of falling titbits. From time to time the chief flung a tiny portion of fish or ncima to one side and there was an immediate scrambled fight as they all struggled to reach it first.

As always, we ate with our fingers and while we did so, the chief wondered what an elderly white man was doing walking through his territory. He didn't put it quite like that, but I could see the concern in his eyes. I tried to explain my motives and asked if he knew about the devastating logging taking place in the area.

He nodded gravely and told me that permits were issued by government in Maputo and he had no control over what was happening. The only reward that he and his people had received from the logging operation was the building of the school, for which he was very grateful.

He went on to say that all three of us looked very tired and suggested that we stay with him for a couple of days. We were indeed starting to flag a bit and I promised to think on his offer and let him know the following day.

That night, I took a long time getting to sleep. The Chinese logging operations had upset me, but Africa has always suffered with the problem of instant utilisation. Little thought is ever given to future needs and if something will give immediate benefit, then it is instantly used.

I recalled a story told to me by a Zambian farming friend. A magnificent palm tree had been cut down on the farm and when asked why, those responsible for the cutting had indicated a bee hive in the top of the tree.

"We needed the honey," was the explanation and I could identify with that. When one is hungry and life is difficult, it is not easy to think ahead to the needs of tomorrow, next week or next year. Immediate problems need immediate solutions and – as with the probable fate of fish stocks in Lake Cabora Bassa – the future is not provided for.

I didn't suppose it was a problem native to Africa and felt that the same difficulties would occur wherever life was hard and simple. Moffat and Isiah hadn't really understood my anguish at the decimating of Mopani forest, but that to me was far more heinous than sating instant needs. The Chinese are systematically raping the environment of wild Africa and the consequences can only be appalling. Once the Mopani forest disappears, a huge swathe of Mozambique will rapidly become desert.

My soul burned with impotent rage.

I did fall asleep eventually but woke in the early hours with my teeth chattering and my entire body shivering with the cold. A feeling of panic threatened to engulf me. It had to be the malaria again and I thought back to Doctor Trishie's warning as to what would happen if I suffered another attack of the dread disease. Despite its kindly chieftain, I didn't really want to die in Nyansorro.

I was still alive in the morning, but my teeth were chattering like runaway piano keys. Wrapping myself in my blanket, I wandered outside to find Moffat blowing furiously on the remains of a fire.

"Eeish that was a cold night, Boss." He greeted and I felt a surge of relief that it was the weather that had disturbed my sleep, not malaria bugs. Later the chief told me that such sudden temperature drops were not unusual in Nyansorro and that it would be warm again the next night.

He was right too and not for the first time, I marvelled at the unpredictability of African travel.

The village livestock were let out of their stockades at first light and it was fascinating to watch them being fed. They all ate the same food and it was put in a long wooden trough which they crowded around. Goats, pigs, chickens, three ducks and a few guinea fowl squabbled and pushed to get at the food, watched closely by at least seven mangy looking dogs that made no effort to interfere. When the meal was over, each breed got themselves together and went off to do whatever it was they did, seemingly getting on well despite the cackling animosities of feeding time.

With the fire blazing, I pushed myself closer to it with a cup of tea and was soon joined by all the dogs and half a dozen blanket-wrapped children. They crowded together, obviously getting warmth from each other as well as the fire. When the flames died down, one of the little mites would be off into the bush and return with a log to get the blaze going again.

Later in the day I asked Chiefy – I couldn't call him by his full Mozambican nomenclature – how many children he had and he rather proudly told me that there were twenty. I was surprised at this, but he smilingly explained that they were from four wives, the one who had cooked our fish meal being number four. Calling her out of the kitchen hut, he introduced her as Mariasinha Notissi. She curtsied in traditional African manner and she also asked me about my adventures. Unlike most rural African women, she didn't seem cowed or overawed by her menfolk and I had the feeling that this was a strong lady indeed.

This was confirmed later when Chiefy held court among a few of his subjects. Although I couldn't understand a word of what went on and my tame interpreter had gone off to play football, there was a simple dignity about proceedings that impressed me. Chiefy sat in a tattered deck chair with a table in front of him while the supplicants huddled together on a bench opposite. Mariasinha watched over proceedings from a shady spot under the eaves of her hut and occasionally would interrupt with what seemed to be pertinent words. When she spoke, proceedings ceased and the entire Court would turn to listen to her pronouncements.

Watching it all from a chair set up outside my tent, I was impressed with Chiefy's handling of everything. Although he was dressed in torn clothing, covered by a huge brown coat – he had worn the same outfit the previous day – he spoke quietly but with great authority. With his permission, I took a few photographs, but didn't dare take the one that might have proved best of the lot. Late in the morning, there was a lull in visitations and Chiefy leaned back in his chair, put gnarled bare feet up on the table and smoked a hand-rolled cigarette.

There were no airs and graces with this particular ruler. He did surprise me though when I asked his age. Producing a folded registration certificate from a voluminous pocket, he pointed to the date of birth. He had been born in nineteen thirty-one which made him well into his eighties and thirteen years older than me. No wonder the man had dignity.

Moffat had arranged porters for the following morning but by seven thirty, they hadn't arrived and Mariasinha insisted that we have breakfast. It was hot by the time that was over, so it didn't take much of an invitation from Chiefy for me to spend another day in his village. It was a pleasant place and he was a nice man. Moffat and Zaire had quite a long trek to get water from a well, but they didn't seem to mind and usually went off with a gaggle of giggling young women to accompany them.

The day followed a similar pattern to the previous one and I felt the aches and pains accumulated over the past few weeks begin to ease. When our porters arrived the following day and we were ready to leave, I handed out fish hooks and needles, plus a couple of packets of sweets that I had bought the previous day. The sweets were for Chiefy's numerous children. I wasn't sure how many of them were still living at home, but there were a lot of them. Everyone thanked me gravely and I walked on with my own little entourage, feeling that I had made new friends and met a truly dignified ruler of people.

As I write this, I listen with dismay to the childish squabbling of western politicians and leaders on issues that are not really important and can't help feeling that so called civilisation has eroded so much that is decent from the human species.

Modern politicians can learn a great deal from the tribal rulers of rural Africa.

* * *

We had been informed by Chiefy that we were twenty-eight kilometres from Nyakafula and unless we left the road for the river, there were no water sources before then. It was a lengthy trek and I wondered if my two days off were going to prove beneficial after all.

My doubts increased when I met the porters, Moffat had hired. We were paying them a hundred meticais apiece rather than the usual fifty, but Robert looked older than me while the younger man, Florinda seemed little more than a child. When I queried their ages, Robert smilingly told me that he had been born in nineteen forty, so that made him nearly five years my senior. He must have noticed the doubt on my face as he promptly hoisted my heavy pack on to his head and set off at a brisk pace.

This soon tailed off however and unencumbered, I strode on ahead, my little party falling ever further behind. The road surface made for easy walking and I wanted to get as much mileage in as I could before the day heated up and my festering legs started to act up again.

They really were a mess too. The antiseptic cream did not seem to be having any effect and most of my wounds wcre weeping copiously and attracting swarms of flies. I walked slapping away with my handkerchief but this didn't seem to deter them for long. I had started taking a course of anti-biotics a couple of days previously but as yet, these hadn't done anything for mc either.

So I set a cracking pace, only pausing at a small roadside stall where I invested in cool drinks for everyone. Isiah did a little dance in the dust and Moffat decided to show that he was strong and fit by indulging in press ups. Somewhat irritably I told them to sober up and concentrate on walking.

In truth, I was very grumpy at this stage and little things seemed to affect my good humour far more than they should have. Isiah's infectious, high-pitched laugh had been catching at first, but now it grated and Moffat's habit of sniffing loudly really got on my nerves. On many occasions I longed to be back on my own despite the fact that life was so much easier for me with the two of them.

At one point, I suggested to Moffat that Robert and Florinda should exchange packs so that the older man carried the lighter one, but he waved my concerns aside.

"He wants the money so he can earn it," Was his comment and I marvelled at the heartlessness of youth.

The morning seemed to take forever and grew more uncomfortable by the minute. Isiah was carrying our cooking pots and with every step, they clanked together until I felt like yelling at him. Fortunately perhaps, I kept my irritability to myself and tried to block everything from my mind and concentrate on walking. I counted my steps as I went along, feeling a momentary triumph as I crossed off each thousand, but it was a long hot road and as we reached the outskirts of Nyakafula, I breathed a long sigh of relief and called a halt beneath shady roadside trees.

As we sat on our packs, Moffat's phone rang and he handed it to me. It was Mawaya wondering how we were doing and where we were. When I told him, he sounded astonished.

"You must be running," He told me cheerfully. "Keep this up and we will need to tie an anchor to you. You don't have far to go now."

I passed his comment on to my companions and Moffat grinned.

"You were in four-wheel drive today," He informed me. "Now we are all tired again."

There were still a good two hundred and fifty kilometres ahead of us, but Mawaya's call certainly cheered me up. It was comforting to hear a friendly voice and speak English for a change, but we still had walking to do.

Nyakafula was a large, sprawling centre that was a town rather than a village and the government offices were another couple of kilometres further on. I suggested that our porters should be released as they still had a long walk back, but my blokes were adamant that they should earn their money. I think they were both a little aggrieved that I had consented to the porters receiving double wages for the day. I justified my decision with the argument that twenty-eight kilometres was a long way to walk on one day, but my two were not impressed.

So we trudged on into the heat of the afternoon, but the fact that we had reached our immediate goal gave me that little extra strength I so desperately needed.

It was late afternoon when we staggered into the town council offices and an ascetic looking man glanced up at our entrance, his eyes wide with obvious surprise. Alberto Benz was the council secretary and dressed in an impeccable white suit that put our torn and dusty clothing to shame.

He listened carefully to our story and when I asked whether there was somewhere to stay that didn't entail further walking, he smilingly showed us to a thatched shelter outside the offices. It was surrounded by open ground and he said that travellers usually stayed there and that we would not have to pay for the privilege.

First though, we needed to check in with the Governor who was a jovial fellow and commented admiringly on my very obvious age. He laughed uproariously when I told him that we were walking to Chinde and directed us to the police station, just in case we were 'travelling criminals.'

The cops were not so friendly and a young and very officious officer accompanied us back to the council offices, where he meticulously went through every item in our still unpacked luggage. It was a laborious business as we had to explain what everything was. He wrote it all down and I was beginning to feel intensely irritated by the rigmarole. I was tired and thirsty, but struggled to hold on to my temper.

It was Alberto who brought it to an end by appearing from his office and speaking sharply to the policeman who immediately ended his inspection. I had no idea what had been said, but I smiled my thanks to the secretary. He went on to hesitantly explain that although there were three water pumps close to where we were camped, they were all producing brackish water at the time so we would have to walk a further two kilometres for clean water. Thankfully I sent Moffat and Isiah back to do the necessary while I sat somewhat forlornly on my pack.

While they were away, I was visited by Chief Cephas of the Nyakafula District and he like all the other chiefs we had encountered was easy going and welcoming. He had a little English, so we chatted awhile before he headed off into the gathering darkness on his motor bike. I didn't want food and was happy to crawl into my tent and let my overtaxed muscles relax.

It had been a very long and wearying day but before I dropped off to sleep, I spared a thought for the two unfortunate porters who even then were plodding back to Nyansorro.

There were certainly times when life on the road was anything but fun.

My two cut throats were keen to spend the following day in Nyakafula but I had the bit between my teeth now and was anxious to press on. I was worrying about my festering legs too as I was sure the constant bombardment by neighbourhood flies was going to lead to further trouble. The anti-biotics didn't appear to be helping and I felt that I probably needed medical attention. Nyakafula had a small clinic, but it was right on the other side of town and I did not want to go backward for any reason.

So after coffee and a bun, we were on the road again, Moffat and Isiah looking distinctly mutinous, but I was in a hurry now. We were apparently thirty-five kilometres from Nyakoro which was the next major town and I wanted to get there as soon as I could.

I also wanted to get off the road and back to the Zambezi, but it seemed as though we were travelling ever further inland which was adding distance to my walk. This was not ideal and I kept urging my companions to get us back to the river, but I think they preferred the easier walking, even if it meant travelling further. Eventually I threw a tantrum and told them both that my task was to walk the length of the 'Zambezi bloody River,' not sample the high life of Mozambican towns. Their task was to help me reach the end of my walk and if they were not going to do that, I would put them on a bus and send them back to Tete. I don't think I stamped my foot, but my language was probably a bit more colourful than what I have written here.

My fit of bad temper did the trick too and the following day, Moffat and Isiah were up and ready to go long before I was – something unheard of on the trip so far. I still set a hard pace and whenever we stopped for a rest, my companions would lie flat on their backs and try to sleep. I couldn't afford to do that however or I might never have stood up again, so at rest breaks, I prowled fitfully around, envying the younger men their ability to take advantage of any situation.

Nyakoro was the largest centre we had passed through since leaving Tete. There were cars, lorries and motor bikes everywhere and it felt strange to be surrounded by traffic. We arrived half way through the morning and I gazed around in some wonderment. Double storey buildings abounded and a few of the streets were tarred. Most of the buildings had flags outside them and I presumed these were government offices. Mind you, flags flew proudly in many of the tiny villages we had walked past and although a number of these were the official Mozambique emblem, there were also some that were unidentifiable. Personal standards perhaps or maybe the signs of obscure political parties. There was a general election due in September so there was already a great deal of patriotic fervour in the rural areas.

There was a large market operating in the centre of Nyakoro and I bought myself some soft socks as the only ones I owned – I had inadvertently left a pair at Benga – were beginning to fall apart. My next port of call was a telephone shop. They didn't have the relevant batteries for my little Chinese phone, but phones themselves were relatively inexpensive so I purchased a pink and white number that I was assured would last me for ever.

Then it was off to the police station to check in and ask where we could camp. The station consisted of a sprawling set of offices and well-tended lawns leading down to the river. It was nearly a week since we had last seen the Zambezi so it felt good to be back.

We were greeted by a young constable who spoke excellent English. His name was Elias Martinho and he took me through to the man in charge who sat behind a wide desk and carried officer pips on his shoulder. His name was Lorenzo and he was not as welcoming as had been his subordinate. In fact, he grilled me at length, examining my papers and asking unanswerable questions as to my reasons for being in his town and how long it would take me to reach the sea. He harped at length on the fact that I write for a living and I reflected that although we scribblers are looked on with some respect in the western world, in Africa anyone who writes is invariably regarded with deep suspicion.

I did my best to remain unflustered and laughed when he asked whether I was a spy for a foreign government.

"What government would employ a man of my age as a spy," I scoffed but he was deadly serious.

"It is an excellent disguise" He said. "Perhaps you are not as old as you look."

Trying hard not to be offended by his paranoia, I pointed to my passport that he was holding.

"That will tell you how old I am."

"Ah, but passports can be forged. You might have bought this in Beira or Maputo."

And so it went on. Lorenzo was determined to find something wrong and we sat uncomfortably in his office for well over an hour. A CID or Special Branch officer was called in but he took one look at me and left with a dismissive wave. Lorenzo was not as easy to satisfy and continued his aggressive questioning.

"You must go and get a permit to stay from the Governor's office," He decided eventually. "Martinho will show you the way."

Off we went again and I was expecting another grilling, but we were greeted by a genial young man called Joel Linha. He laughed when I told him of my interview with the surly cop and assured me that I needed no governor's permit to stay in Nyakoro. He didn't like the idea of us camping by the river though and escorted us to a deserted compound behind the police station. It was relatively clean and there was a huge tree under which my tent could be placed, so I was happy enough with his choice.

It was also close to the fleshpots of Nyakoro for my two companions, so Moffat and Isiah were also pleased with our new home. We had been through a hard few days and my newly purchased phone required a lot of charging, so I made them even happier by decreeing that we would spent the next day in Nyakoro as well.

Martinho and Joel visited us again that afternoon and I questioned the former about his police career. It had only lasted three years at that stage and for two of those, he had been stationed in Nyakoro.

"There is nothing to do here," He told me sadly. "There are no married quarters and my wife and two year old son are in Chimoio. That is four hundred kilometres away so I do not often see them. I have repeatedly asked to be transferred, but I am too junior for the big bosses to worry about."

How often have I heard similar tales of woe from coppers I worked with? Policemen are part of the civil service whatever country they operate in and civil service rules are seldom favourable toward serving officers.

But he was a nice young man was Elias Martinho and when we parted, he gave me his telephone number 'in case I ever needed help.'

Joel made life seem infinitely better when he told me that from here to the sea, there was a track that led directly along the path of the Zambezi.

"You cannot miss it and it will be easy to follow."

That was a boost to my flagging morale and I told Moffat and Isiah that from now on, we were not following any roads. I should have known better. Rural Africans are truly kind people and will invariably tell a stranger what they think he wants to hear.

Another visitor to our strange little camp was a hard-eyed CID man called Horace. He wouldn't tell me his other name, but he came from Chinde, so this time I was asking the questions. He was not too sanguine as to my chances of reaching the place however and at one point, looked at my legs and asked how I could walk that far.

"You are damaged and soon the poison will spread. How can you possibly walk all that way?"

I didn't know to be honest, but I assured him that I would make it.

Horace wanted his photograph taken but would not allow me to take it with the police station as a backdrop, so it had to be in bad light beside my tent. I don't know what it is about Africa, but officialdom seems almost paranoid about anyone taking photographs of buildings, however innocent they may be.

Before starting out on the second leg of my Zambezi Walk, I had learned that an old friend of mine and his wife ran a safari lodge in a place called Caia. This was on my proposed route to the sea. Caia was still some distance away, but I felt that we needed a little comfort in our lives to keep us going. Although our camps were reasonably pleasant, they were invariably very basic and didn't really afford us the rest that we needed. There were times when I longed for a hot shower or to be able to click a switch and have light. I wanted to experience sleeping in a bed again or lounging in a comfortable armchair. I had telephone numbers for Ant and Pat White, so once my new phone was up and going, sent them text messages asking whether we could stop over at their lodge when we reached Caia.

My messages went unanswered and so I contacted Deborah's friend, Kevin Pitzer who had so kindly flown me to Johannesburg when the cerebral malaria had hit me. He was also a friend of the Whites, so I checked my phone numbers with him and asked whether he could pass my query on. He came back to me a day or so later to say that Ant and Pat were away for a few weeks, but I was welcome to spend a few days at the lodge and Kevin's company would foot the bill.

This was unbelievably generous of Kevin and it gave us the

prospect of a little genuine comfort to look forward to. It was with a much lighter heart that I left Nyakoro after two nights in our funny little compound. Moffat was limping now, having joined in a football match with Isiah and a group of children. Playing without shoes, he had miskicked the ball and his right foot had split and was quite swollen. I sympathised but warned him that I intended to keep on at the same cruel pace. I was becoming desperate to get my walk over. He would just have to do what I had done when my feet were sore – walk in sandals.

My legs were fast becoming a serious problem and I had to get them seen to. Even the CID man had noticed the way they were red and festering. There was a small hospital in Nyakoro and I asked Moffat to get me some more antiseptic cream as mine was running out. Off he went but returned looking crestfallen as apparently Isiah had pretended that the cream was for him and then hadn't been able to display the need for it when required to do so. The pair of them had been chased out of the hospital. I didn't have the energy to walk there myself and didn't think it would do any good in any case. Moffat and Isiah would probably be chased away again and without them to interpret, nobody would understand my problem in any case. I resolved to wait for my antiseptic cream, but knew that I couldn't keep ignoring the problem of my legs. They looked disgusting and were making me feel quite sick.

CHAPTER FIFTEEN
(Towns, Troubles and a Pretty Girl)

Two evenings later, I was sitting outside my tent, gazing morosely into a fire. This time of day was normally peacefully pleasant, but I was in another foul mood. The day had started fairly well and for an hour and a half we had followed a path from which we had numerous sightings of the Mighty Zambezi. Progress was good but the path wound around a great deal and whenever we came to a fork, Moffat and Isiah would argue as to which track to take. Had I been on my own, I would have stuck to the side closer to the river, but my two lads were townies and seemed very fearful of getting lost.

In the bush that is an attitude that cannot work and all too soon, we were lost and I was cross again. I had been enjoying my morning until then and grunted to Moffat that I would make all future decisions. Off we went again and on the edge of a wide inlet, we encountered a fishermen laying out his nets to dry. A long chat ensued and in the course of it, he gave us a little demonstration of throwing his net across the water. Very impressive it was too but I was anxious to move on.

"He will show us where to go Boss," Moffat assured me and as we walked on, I had the feeling that we were heading in entirely the wrong direction. My fears were confirmed when we came out of the bush to find ourselves on another wide road, this one complete with a long line of bancas and noisy beer halls.

I made my feelings known to Moffat, but again I did not want to go backward, so I trudged on down the road feeling that nothing was going quite to plan.

As I said, my companions were both townies and both gregarious fellows, so they preferred being with other people and walking in comparative comfort to moving with difficulty through unyielding foliage on narrow paths. I on the other hand was becoming ever more anti-social and did not want to mix with people or answer the interminable questions that were thrown at me when we were in public. It was unreasonable, but it was also a very real problem.

My legs had taken another bashing and blood joined the pus that was already trickling down both calves. This horrible mixture was pure manna to the flies and I knew that they would be spreading infection to any new scratches. After a few kilometres I called a halt, took out my first aid pack and wrapped both legs in crepe bandages that were blindingly white. I knew they wouldn't stay like that for long, but I must have presented a weird sight with both legs cocooned to the knee in crepe.

Around midday we walked somewhat listlessly through Kondonga Village and I called a halt. We set up camp in a patch of cheerless bush outside the village and I took my Kindle out to read. I had been engrossed in a biblical novel about Ben Hur but when I switched the Kindle on, nothing happened. I knew there was plenty of life in the battery, but the little machine had died on me and nothing I did produced even a spark of life.

This was another bitter blow. I had stood on a Kindle during my walk through Zambia and bought another one for the second half of my journey. That had mysteriously packed up on me while I staggered around Cabora Bassa but Shelagh Brown had loaned me hers when I stayed on Cherry Farm. I had been reluctant to take responsibility for the machine, but she waved my objections aside.

"If it breaks then it breaks," She said practically and now it had. I felt very bad and dreaded having to tell her, but my main worry was that I couldn't remember the name of the story and I had nothing to read for however many weeks I still had to walk.

That third Kindle added to an impressive list of items of kit that I had lost or broken during my Zambezi Walk. Three cameras, four pipes. Two dictaphones and a GPS. Now three Kindles and I didn't know why. Standing on one was obviously not the thing to do, but the latter two – as with two of the cameras - had just stopped working. It was probably due to the incredible heat, but sometimes it felt as though a malevolent spirit was dogging my footsteps.

After wrestling with the recalcitrant Kindle for a while, I irritably sent Moffat and Isiah into the village to find water, but they returned waterless and with an obviously angry little man in tow. This was the village headman, Antonino Benza and my worthy henchman sadly announced that Antonino didn't want us anywhere near his village as we 'looked like dangerous people.'

It would have been easy enough to pack up and move on, but as I said, I was in a foul mood. Mr Benza was obviously very drunk and he shouted at all three of us in his own language. Even Isiah was having difficulty in following it and suddenly I snapped.

"Shuddup!" I roared and nearby goats looked up in surprise. "Instead of ranting at us like that, tell me quietly why you object to our presence."

My change in tone obviously made an impression and after a momentary pause, Antonino walked right up to me, took my arm in his and started leading me away. He smiled widely at me and the waft of already consumed native beer almost made me stagger. He was still talking at great speed but in a quieter tone and Isiah muttered something to Moffat.

"He wants you to go back to his house Boss," That came as a surprise. "He says you are a great man and he wants you to meet his family."

Kondonga was a modern village with brick houses on both sides of the road and Antonino lived in the first of these. It was pleasantly painted and chickens rooted happily around in a small back garden. The front door was magnificently carved and had a startlingly red handle. I was probably being unfair, but my immediate thought was that it had been a legacy of the Portuguese occupation and Antonino had added the handle himself. His attitude toward me had completely changed and through Isiah, he asked whether we needed water, as the nearest well was always crowded and the river was three kilometres away.

When I told him that we did need some, he clapped his hands and ordered what was obviously a daughter to fill up a bucket. All the while this was being done, he kept up a continual monologue and I shrugged at Isiah who did a limited translation through Moffat.

"He is very pleased to be able to assist you Boss," That worthy announced with a huge grin. "He is proud that you have decided to sleep in Kondonga Village."

That was a turn up for the books and it surely wasn't my charm that had brought about the abrupt change in mood for the little headman. However, we took the bucket back to camp and I was even able to shave for the first time in a while.

That evening I switched on my pink and white telephone to find two text messages waiting for me. One was the inevitable 'Go Madala Go' from Alex the Rasta and the other was from Karien Kermer, who had been so good to me in Livingstone. She told me that ZDF German Television were in Livingstone making part of a major documentary on the Zambezi. They wanted to film the finish of my walk and would be in Chinde on the first of October to do so.

That immediately added to my bad mood. Mfanasibili Nkosi (it didn't sound very German) of ZDF had contacted me many weeks previously and asked if they could send a cameraman to accompany me. I had turned him down flat but said the company could film me crossing into Mozambique or at the finish if they really wanted. They hadn't appeared at Feira or Zumbu and now they were setting a timetable for me to adhere to. At the rate I was travelling I would reach Chinde well before October and I had no intention of slowing down or waiting for them to arrive.

I sent angry messages to both Karien and my daughter Deborah who had also been speaking to Mr Nkosi. I told them both that I would liaise again when I was close to Chinde and give them a date for my arrival, but I was sticking to my own timetable. I have always been scornful of television adventurers and had no intention of tailoring my walk to suit anyone else.

I dropped off that night feeling very disgruntled with life. My last diary entry for the day read 'Tomorrow can only be better.'

* * *

In fact, the day started well. We left camp shortly after first light and I was setting a stiff pace, but when an exceedingly pretty young lady cycled by, Moffat shouted something after her. Turning in her saddle, she gave him the sort of look that makes young men all over the world go weak at the knees. A shy wave followed and then she was gone.

"What did you say to her?" I queried and he smiled.

"I asked her why she wasn't around last night."

That little episode cheered us all up and we walked on with a spring in our steps.

Later in the day, we had stopped for a rest some way off the road and I watched as a little family cycled by. Mom was in front with a toddler behind her and Dad followed with a boy of about eight clinging on for dear life. Seeing me some forty metres away, the father brought his bike to a halt, climbed off and waved cheerily. I waved back and he went on, making me feel that perhaps Mozambican villagers were not as stand offish as I had thought.

As if to balance the equation, in one village we encountered another drunk who was decidedly unfriendly. He had a bottle of gin in one hand and a bottle of beer in the other and on spotting me, he started shouting. I couldn't understand what he was saying, but the words, 'bloody ma English' certainly stood out, particularly as he kept repeating them with ever more venom.

Moffat looked embarrassed and I didn't ask for a translation. The sentiment behind the tirade had been pretty obvious and I wondered vaguely why he hated the English when it was the Portuguese who had colonised his country.

The drunken man – it was barely ten in the morning – followed us for a while and although I wasn't running away from him, our pace noticeably picked up until we left him behind. Incidents like that had been rare during my months of walking but they always leave a nasty taste in the mouth.

By midday we were all very tired and the temperature was well into the forties but Moffat reckoned that we were very close to Charamba, another major centre, so we kept going. Eventually I told him to ask a couple of lady villagers how far we actually were from the centre and they told us that we would get there by the evening. That was enough for me and pulling off the road, we made camp. It was always nice when we covered a good distance during a day, but I had no intention of killing myself. At that stage, I calculated that if we only did ten kilometres a day, we would reach the ocean in mid-September and that was fine by me.

But we were averaging well in excess of ten kays per day and I could see that my companions were feeling the strain as much as I was. I kept telling myself to slow down, but there was always that lurking fear that something would happen to wreck my walk, so I had to get as far as I could before it did.

Looking back so many months later, I find it very strange. I was not afraid of the people I was walking among; I was not afraid of wild life or snakes; I was not afraid of officialdom, but I was afraid of failing in what I had set out to do.

It all seemed very odd, even to me.

* * *

Days merged into days and villages into villages. There were large ones and small ones; some of them were memorable for one thing or another, others were entirely forgettable. The big difference they had from similar villages in Zambia was that none of them had a restaurant. In Zambia, any large conurbation had at least one – sometimes merely a hut with tables outside, but here we had to forage and cook for ourselves. Moffat did most of it, although occasionally Isiah had a go but his meals were barely edible.

I hated being on a road, but occasionally we saw the Zambezi. In Nyakapona Village, we were sat outside a small store and I was approached by a young man called Bizique who spoke excellent English. He was a Malawian and told me that he could not find employment in Mozambique. Did I know whether he would get a job if he went to Zimbabwe or Zambia? I didn't but we had an interesting conversation and once again, it was nice to speak English.

For probably the first time since I had arrived in Mozambique, I was 'blessed' by my interlocutor who commented that God must have been looking after me. I agreed that he certainly had and Bizique told me that God must love me very much.

I had become accustomed to religious rhetoric in Zambia and felt almost nostalgic at the young man's words. The bush makes one very conscious of a Deity or Higher Being and it was nice to be reminded of it once again.

Bizique showed us a lovely spot to camp beside the river and I felt my frustration ease as I looked out over that wonderful stretch of water. It was an excellent camp and I wandered around the surrounding countryside, revelling in the riverine vegetation, rather than the Mopani forest, we seemed to have walked through for ages.

In one spot I found a large tree, festooned with woven rush mats. A little further on there was another tree similarly adorned and I wondered if this was some way of propitiating the Gods of fishing.

Apparently not: I tasked my reprobates with finding out and they returned with the news that there was a lunatic in the area who spent his time weaving the mats then hanging them on trees. Nobody – not even he – could explain why.

In another village I spent my Saturday afternoon watching a group of girls playing a strange kind of ball game. They used a tennis ball sized sphere made from plastic bags and string. Two of them stood about twelve metres apart and a volunteer would then stand between them. They threw the ball at her with squeals of glee and if it hit the target, she would retire and another one took her place. That was easy enough to follow but when the ball missed its target, the girl in the middle would scoop up a handful of sand and place it on a pile. I wasn't sure what that meant and there was nobody to ask as Moffat had wandered off and Isiah had managed to get himself a game of football. Where he found the energy after days of covering twenty-five kilometres or more, I just couldn't imagine.

Charamba, which Moffat had been so keen to reach proved to be a desolate, litter-strewn town that stank to high heaven. The houses were built of brick, but most of them looked derelict and there was nothing to recommend the place so we marched on through. On Mawaya's route instruction sheet, he had listed the next target as Sena and estimated that it was seventy kilometres further on. We had walked through Charamba and on for another hour and we came to a road sign telling us that Sena was eighty-five kays away and that knocked my ever more fragile confidence for a loop. We were all desperately tired, Moffat and Isiah had taken to bickering among themselves and I knew that I was acting quite boorishly toward the pair of them.

I felt that we just had to keep moving and I longed to get off the road and back beside the river.

At Nyakapona I had described in my diary how different the river people were from those who lived inland. Beside the Zambezi, everyone was friendly and welcoming, but in the roadside villages people – with a few exceptions – were wary and unapproachable.

There also seemed far more drunks inland and we encountered more than our fair share of them.

But we seemed to be committed to seeing the Mighty Zambezi only every few days and I plodded on, cursing myself, my companions, the people around me and the very idea of walking the ruddy Zambezi.

It was not a happy few days and as we approached the little town of Chema, disaster struck.

When we started out that morning, Moffat complained that his back was very sore and my heart sank into my boots. It was an occupational hazard that walking many kilometres with a heavy pack would lead to back trouble, but we still had a long way to go and I needed both my porters.

I urged him on and we made fitful progress through the morning. Every half an hour or so Moffat needed a rest and I didn't want to make things worse by forcing him on. As far as I could judge we were only a few kilometres from Chema and although my worthy henchman was looking a bit green around the gills, I felt that we needed to get there as soon as we could. Perhaps they would have a clinic where we could stock up on pain killers – and of course, antiseptic cream for my battered legs.

Kilometre by painful kilometre we plodded along. A group of jovial women told us that we had less than two kays to go and that gave us a boost, but Moffat suddenly turned a strange grey colour and told me that he felt very cold. His teeth were chattering and my worst fear had come about. He obviously had malaria.

This was serious and I took over a heavier pack while poor old Isiah carried two, allowing the now obviously ill Moffat to stagger on unencumbered. Fortunately, we were able to flag down a motor cyclist and asked him to take Moffat to the nearest clinic. Off they went with my not-very-well Number Two waving us a feeble farewell.

When we finally arrived in the little town, we discovered that they had more than a clinic. Moffat had been taken to a proper hospital and was being seen by a doctor. This was good news, but it was not so good when the doctor came out to tell us that Moffat definitely had malaria, was being treated with Coartem and would have to stay in for at least a night.

That left me in a complete quandary. We would have to stay in Chema and the hospital staff could only suggest a flea pit called the PITXI –PITXIS. What that meant, I had no idea but the place would not have won stars for comfort in any society. It was brick built and had spasmodic electricity but there was no water, despite my room having a spectacularly smart shower cubicle. All I could do was gaze at it somewhat wistfully.

We spent the best part of three days in that little hell hole and without anything to read, they were long days indeed. Chema was a reasonably clean place and compared favourably with similar centres such as Senanga in Zambia but nothing seemed to work. It had obviously been a garrison town in Portuguese days and we had passed an abandoned fort on the way in. There was an old cannon mounted on a plinth outside the hospital and I felt a huge sense of sadness that everything was being allowed to decay.

Mind you, the PI – whatever it was called - did have a thatched bar in the courtyard so I was able to have a couple of cold beers which helped my mood a little. It didn't serve food however and I eventually decided that it was probably the local brothel. At eight o'clock the following morning there were a load of drunken men wandering around with beers in their hands and a lot of them had heavily made up women hanging on to them.

To each his own I suppose and it certainly wasn't the first time I had slept in such an establishment.

What amazed me though was that beer was kept chilled, there was a television in the bar, but water had to be taken from buckets. It must have originally come from a pump somewhere, so surely it would not have been a problem to have it piped through to the town itself. I presumed it was the same situation everywhere in Chema, but I suppose it could have just pertained to the PITI Whatever.

I had a bit of a personal shock before going to bed that evening. No longer needing to pee in the bush, I used the ornate but run down bathroom and did my thing in a proper toilet – with attendant water bucket of course. My urine was red with blood and I wondered what this signified. Fortunately perhaps, there was a telephone signal, so I sent a text to Shelagh Brown in Ndola and asked her to find out for me. She contacted Irish Eliz, a former nurse who said that it could be reaction to the anti-biotics I had been taking or it could be the prelude to another bout of malaria.

I wasn't feeling particularly well but had put it down to worried frustration at the situation. But to be safe, I began yet another course of Coartem and prayed that it would ward off any more malaria.

Moffat came out of hospital the following morning and professed himself ready and willing to start again right away. He immediately demonstrated his fitness by performing ten press ups on the pavement, but I told him that he was going to spend the night – and possibly the next one – with us in the flea pit. I didn't mention that I wasn't feel too good myself!

I sent the two of them off to find somewhere to eat and spent much of the day on the fleapit veranda watching the citizenry of Chema going about their daily business. It seemed a busy little town and everyone was friendly, but I was anxious to move on and get away from civilisation again. This was too modern with tarmac streets and abundant traffic. I longed for the bush, quiet camps and my lovely river.

A downside to my vigil was that the most common form of transport going through the town was heavy lorries carrying massive logs. I counted twenty-five of the ruddy things before giving up and cursing the Chinese for raping my beloved continent.

We ate well that night, the Chaps having found a proper restaurant on the road out of town. I had chicken and rice while the other two accompanied their chicken with ncima. Seeing pork chops on the menu, I decided that we should have breakfast the following day and ordered pork chops and rice for breakfast. Silly me! We arrived in the morning, only to be told that the chops had not yet arrived, so chicken and rice it was again.

We were still thirty odd kilometres from Sena and I worried that neither Moffat nor I might make it. He suggested that we take a bus and somewhat reluctantly – I felt it was cheating – I agreed, so after breakfast, off we went in proper transport.

Buses in Mozambique are not like buses elsewhere. Here they were open trucks, crammed with as many bodies in the back as they can possibly fit in. I well remembered watching one in a village after

Nyakafula. It had people hanging over the side, people on the roof and bicycles slung at the rear. How they all stayed in place I had no idea and they were heading back to Nyakafula (a five hour drive) late in the evening. If a passenger fell off, nobody would know but I suppose that is bus travel in Mozambique. You pay your money and you take the risk.

Another disadvantage with African bus travel is that the vehicle only sets out when it has enough passengers to make it worthwhile. We waited most of the morning in Chema but eventually off we went. I was wedged between an old lady with chickens in a basket on her lap and a comely wench who was firmly pressed against me.

It was not a comfortable ride, but eventually we arrived in Sena (more properly Vila de Sena) none the worse for wear. It was not an inviting place but it was close to the river and we made an uncomfortable camp beside the Zambezi. From the camp we could see the magnificent Dona Ana railway bridge. Built by the Portuguese in nineteen thirty-four, this splendid edifice was over three and a half kilometres long and had thirty-three eighty-metre spans and seven spans of fifty metres. It is the longest railway bridge in Africa and although it was rendered unusable by the Rhodesian SAS during the bush war, it had been repaired by the United States aid programme and was back in business. Even as we set up camp, we saw a long goods train trundling across the bridge and there were others throughout the day.

Before we went to bed that night, Moffat asked me whether I was going to sleep once I got into my tent. I told him that I wasn't sure and at about eight o'clock I heard him on the phone to somebody. He spoke in English and complained about the fact that I was pushing them along too fast and showing no consideration for their feelings. I don't normally eavesdrop on other peoples' calls, but this was worrying. He ended the call after a long tirade about my deficiencies by saying, "Don't tell anyone it was me who told you this."

I felt terrible disappointment at his disloyalty. He and Isiah had volunteered to come along but this was my walk, nobody else's.

The following morning, I asked Moffat who he had been calling and he said it was only his wife. That was a blatant lie because he had spoken in English and I had heard him call his wife before. I carefully pointed this out and he looked abashed, but I went on to give the pair of them a choice. They could take a bus back to Tete and I would go on alone or they could carry on with me. I pointed out that I was in charge and they would have to do as I wanted without demur or they could go back. I was not going to give them the choice again.

Without hesitation, they both decided that they would continue with me and I declared the matter closed. I hadn't enjoyed it but I didn't want dissent in the ranks. Caia and a rest was only a few days ahead of us and we all needed that. We started out again and made good time although – inevitably perhaps – we soon found ourselves back on a road.

After another very uncomfortable camp where our water stocks were low, we walked on and around noon, we entered the outskirts of Caia where we stopped for lunch and a beer at a real restaurant. My bandaged legs caused comment from a big chap on the next table and when I explained the problem, he laughed and told me that anyone who walked in the bush was mad because there were too many flies.

Slightly sourly I agreed and we camped that night in a deep *vlei* not far off the road. Kevin had given me the phone number of a lady called Mandy who was running Ant White's lodge at Capatu. I rang her first thing the next morning and she promised to send a truck for us, only asking which side of the bridge we would be. I had thought the lodge would be to the north, so told her that we would wait for her at that end and off we went to cross Caia bridge.

This was another magnificent structure and I reflected that the bridge builders of Mozambique had really excelled themselves. Built in the year, two thousand and eight and over two kilometres long, the Caia bridge is the longest road bridge across the Zambezi. There was a pedestrian path to one side and a small government post where we presented our documents and were waved through. We joined a long string of pedestrians and I was amused to see one young lady, very smartly dressed and carrying a large handbag. Sticking out of the bag was a chicken's foot and from time to time, the handbag emitted an irritated cluck, presumably at the roughness of the ride.

At the other end, was a wide road with what appeared to be a derelict store on one side. We set up camp on the veranda of this and waited for transport and the longed for rest.

CHAPTER SIXTEEN
(Caia and Beyond)

We waited two hours for our lift, but I don't think any of us minded. We were all very weary and my legs were on fire. Isiah was complaining of a headache so appeared likely to be the third of us to go down with malaria within the week. I started him on a course of Coartem as we waited. Both he and Moffat lay down beneath a tree and seemed to sleep but I sat on my veranda and watched the traffic going by.

There were very few motor vehicles, but a constant and colourful stream of pedestrians and cyclists. Many of them were obviously on their way to market somewhere as bikes were loaded with chickens, goats and even a couple of pigs. They wobbled along, the riders shouting greetings to each other and I smiled at the cheerful cacophony of voices.

Burned by the sun over the weeks, I was probably as dark skinned as many of them, but I suppose my clothing and battered bush hat rather set me apart. Many curious looks came my way and one or two people shouted their bom dias in greeting.

At last a small truck hove into view from the southern end of the bridge and the driver turned around on seeing us. I don't know why I had assumed Catapu to be north of the Zambezi but I had been wrong. It is actually some thirty kilometres south of the river, so we had walked a fair few extra kilometres. Still I would not have missed that colourfully exciting morning walk for the world.

Mphingwe Lodge is part of the twenty-five thousand hectare Catapu Timber Estate owned and run by a British Company, TCT Dalman. Situated in a nine and a half thousand hectare game farm, the lodge was rustically comfortable. We were greeted by Mandy Enslin who directed me to a wooden chalet, set apart from the rest, while my two cut throats were housed together at the other end of the camp.

My new home was spacious and comfortable. The windows were gauzed and a large bed beckoned invitingly. More importantly, there was a shower with hot water, something I had not experienced in weeks and I quickly took advantage of it. My horribly dirty clothing was whisked away to be laundered by a smiling maid and I settled in for a couple of restful days. There were books to read, beer to be drunk and the means to make tea or coffee in my room. What more could any weary traveller need?

During the morning I explored the camp and found myself very impressed. It was so nice to be clean, if a little crumpled and in spite of the fact that the area was heavily forested, there were few flies to bother my legs. An open air dining room looked very inviting and although I had turned down the offer of breakfast, I took full advantage of a simple, but delicious lunch.

Isiah was feeling pretty rough and didn't eat that first day which for him was almost unheard of. Moffat and I had dinner together and when he asked for ncima with his main course, it was smilingly prepared. I stuck to potatoes which were another little luxury I had almost forgotten.

Adjacent to the dining room was a lounging area, where a large fire was prepared in the evening for guests to sit around. I bought myself a beer and was joined a little later by Lauren who I think was Mandy's daughter and her husband Leon. As is the way of such meetings, we merely smiled at each other at first, but gradually we started to chat. A young and cheerful couple, they were farming in Chimoio and told me that Mphingwe was their bolthole for peace and quiet whenever they could get away. Mandy's husband Joe joined us and while we talked, he looked with some concern at my legs.

I had taken my bandages off and my festering cuts looked badly inflamed but the cool evening air was soothing and I felt that it had to do me good. Joe told me that scratches becoming infected was commonplace in Mozambican bush areas but assured me that Mandy would know what to do. Later on, she came over to our table and took a good look at my legs.

"It happens to everyone," she pursed her lips, "and there is only one way to cure the sepsis. Have you taken anti biotics?"

I assured her that I had and she offered a novel solution.

"Instead of swallowing the capsules," she told me, "break them in half and sprinkle the powder inside directly on the wounds. That will quickly clear them up I promise. Anyone who walks in the bush has the same problem. This really is a germ-ridden country."

The following morning, she provided me with a card of anti biotic capsules and demonstrated how to extract the powder inside. With my legs liberally coated in white powder, I faced the day with new confidence and within twenty-four hours, the weeping had dried up and my legs felt considerably less painful. Three days later, every one of my scratches was clean and dry. Two years later, I still have the scars to remind me of a simple, but effective way to combat septic sores.

There are times when local remedies are far more effective than those that the drug companies recommend.

We enjoyed three luxurious days at Mphingwe Lodge and I spent a great deal of my time, reflecting on the incredible kindness and generosity I was receiving from people. I had met Kevin Pitzer briefly at my daughter's wedding many years previously. Now, having already spent money and time on flying me to Johannesburg when I needed it, he was paying for three of us to spend time off in luxurious idleness. I knew that Kevin's kindness would have a huge bearing on the ultimate success or failure of my Zambezi Walk and felt humbled that he would go out of his way for me.

There was apparently a great deal of wild life in the forests surrounding the lodge and species to be found included suni, nyala, oribi and bushpig. I took a number of gentle walks around the area but all I saw was a pair of suspicious looking warthogs and a solitary duiker.

I was content though. The forests were cool with little paths meandering through them. I had nothing to carry and nowhere to go so I could switch off and enjoy my surroundings.

I had worried a little about how Moffat and Isiah would cope with a proper dining room and using knives and forks which would seem strange to them. Both of them were accustomed to eating with their fingers. Moffat laughingly coped and Isiah eventually managed to handle the cutlery although he ate off his lap rather than the table.

During my last evening at Mphingwe, I was joined at the fire by a balding man who was travelling through. He looked somewhat curiously at me and asked where I was going. I told him as briefly as I could and suddenly his face lit up.

"I know you," He exclaimed. "You were walking around Lake Kariba many years ago and we met at Sijarira. Do you remember...?"

In fact, I remembered it well. I had been walking from Kariba to Binga for some unknown reason and for the second time in twenty years had stumbled quite inadvertently on beautiful Sijarira Lodge. It had been a Sunday morning and two young chaps had been sitting outside drinking tea as I pottered along a wide, sandy beach. James had been one of them and we spent that evening in Mphingwe pleasantly reminiscing over beer.

"I can remember spotting this skinny apparition coming along the beach and wondering what any person was doing walking in such wild countryside," He told me. "We initially thought you had been shipwrecked or lost."

It had been another magical interlude in a challenging journey and I smiled as I thought back on lovely countryside, abundant wild life and lovely people. Plus of course, lovely food.

Mphingwe – it is named after the local blackwood tree – had been the same and I was sad to climb back in the truck the next morning and return to the bridge at Caia. We still had one hundred and eighty kilometres to walk, but those three days and Mandy's inspired cure for my festering legs had given me the strength to do it and I knew that I would.

I felt sure that nothing could stop me at that stage.

* * *

We had crossed to the northern bank of the river at Caia and with my new found strength and healing legs, it felt good to be back on the Zambezi. What made it even better was that the track we were using actually followed the river and never deviated inland to any degree. It was still hot and the flies were still bad, but Isiah seemed to have completely recovered and was his usual laughing self while Moffat was full of smiles. Between them they must have chatted up every female we passed over the first couple of days.

I left them to their innocent little flirtations – at least I think they were innocent – and set myself a steady pace while I looked around me at the wonderful world that is Africa in the raw.

There had been over one hundred and twenty bird species at Mphingwe and seeing so many of them had made me more aware of my avian neighbours. I have never been a 'bird man' as such, but have always enjoyed their calls, their freedom of flight and their passion for life in the worst of circumstances. In parts of Zambia, they had been all but wiped out by people with catapults, but deep into the Sofala province of Mozambique as we were now, they were all around us.

I spotted a formation of spurwing geese flying upstream as well as bee eaters (I think they were the European variety) and jacanas. Lovebirds and parakeets tweekled in the trees and fish eagles shrieked their challenge to the world. It was noisy but soothing at the same time.

Once again the difference between people living on the river and those inland was very marked. Cheerful 'bom dias' rang out as we passed and women curtsied or clapped their hands behind shy smiles. For the first time in many weeks it felt really good to be alive.

Although we were following what was little more than a path, we were continually stepping aside for motor cycles and I was amused at some of the helmets on display. They varied between full-faced racing jobs to what were little more than industrial hard hats, while the majority of riders went bare headed. One worthy gentleman had what appeared to be a saucepan on his head and he waved cheerfully as Moffat called a greeting.

Over the weeks I had grown used to children running away at our approach and as we approached one small collection of huts, there was a little girl standing in the middle of the path. She was probably about two years old and watched us coming with wide eyes. I waited for her to run, but when I was a couple of metres from her she smiled widely and held her arms out to be hugged.

What could I do but drop my walking pole on the ground and sweep her into my arms. She squealed with laughter and I carried her into the village where everyone was smiling broadly. It was a truly magical moment that will live long in my memory.

I had become accustomed to Moffat introducing me as David

Limao, that being the Portuguese word for Lemon, but suddenly we passed a sign for Limao Village and I wondered how it had earned the name. Unfortunately the sign said that the village was two kilometres inland and that would mean adding four kays to our journey, so I contented myself with a photograph. It might have been an interesting story though.

We spent one hot afternoon camped in a dried out vlei and my blokes went into a sulk because they were running out of mealie meal. At least that was the reason they gave, but I think it was more probable that they wanted to sleep in a village or town rather than the bush.

I was happy though and continued my bird watching. A bird book would have been too heavy to carry, but it might have come in handy. After a lifetime in the bush I can identify quite a few species and during that afternoon, I spotted a yellow-billed kite, a banded goshawk (I think) two coucals, a trumpeter hornbill and a host of 'little brown jobs.' I also enjoyed watching ants and other insects going busily about their daily routine in new grass that was shooting up after a fire.

Towards evening there was a great deal of shouting and a huge man hove into view. He was swinging an axe around his shoulder and was obviously mad as a hatter. Hardly glancing to right or left, he kept up a shouted monologue that seemed to be directed toward the treetops. He glanced briefly at our camp but it didn't seem to make any impression on him. Moving on and still yelling at the heavens, he attacked a large Mopani tree with his axe. When it fell, he lifted it on to his shoulder as though it had been a sapling and walked back the way he had come, still shouting unintelligibly and still swinging the axe. My blokes looked scared but I could only feel sorry for the fellow as I don't suppose he received any psychiatric help.

Mind you, I was pleased that he had used his axe on the Mopani tree rather than us.

The next major centre on our route was Mopeia in Zambezia Province and we walked into town on a blustery Sunday morning. It was another spacious, well laid out centre and we strode down a wide main road, three abreast and probably looking like visiting gunfighters in a spaghetti western. We were short on food at the time, so the first stop was a large and clamorous market. Here we bought the necessary supplies and treated ourselves to coconuts and sweet biscuits. This was definitely the life and I thought without nostalgia back to those horrible days in Zambia when I had lived on my gruel-like health food and longed for something more substantial. Since leaving Tete, I had certainly shed a few pounds, but my ribs weren't sticking out and I felt pretty fit and strong.

After clocking in with the local police station, we crossed the river again and made camp beneath a mango tree amid a lot of garden plots. Women worked in a few of them and looked curiously at us, but I made myself comfortable beneath the tree and prepared for a lazy day. It was Sunday, the weather looked threatening and we had already walked ten kilometres or so that morning.

It might have been a lazy day but it was anything but quiet. Moffat and Isiah went back into town to sound out the scene I suppose and I had a succession of visitors through the morning.

Joseph Kwenje and his son, Francis Joseph came from Malawi and had a smattering of English, so I could chat with them but the majority of my visitors could only speak Portuguese or the local dialect, so all we could do was stare at each other and smile.

As Joseph and his son left me under my tree, they called God's blessing down on my head and said a little prayer asking the Deity to keep 'this brave man' safe. I was touched and wished them well. It seemed that Malawians were as deeply religious as their Zambian counterparts and I wondered why Mozambicans didn't seem the same. After all, their colonial masters had been the very Catholic Portuguese. It was another little anomaly of rural Africa.

It was probably premature of me but I was beginning to worry about the end of my walk. I had just over a hundred kilometres to go and if we carried on at our present pace that was not going to take long. I had been in constant touch with Mawaya and although originally, he had promised that he and Ronnie, possibly with Doug Carlisle would meet me at Luabo and do the final section with me, that had fallen through. Johan now said that he could not reach Chinde before the sixteenth of September and I hoped to be there long before that.

First Quantum Minerals had agreed to send an aircraft to collect me from Chinde, but I had to give them some sort of time scale. I also had to worry about the German film crew so distances and timings went around and round in my head.

I felt I could reach my eventual goal soon after the first of September, even if we slowed right down. It meant that taking days off was no longer a worry, but I still needed to get there before anything went wrong.

We had spoken to the Mopeia police about the way ahead and they had advised that the going outside the town would be impossible if we stuck to the river bank, so it would mean another day or two on roads. They assured me that there was a main road running directly beside the river, but I had heard that story many times before and things had never worked out that way.

Whatever the case, we set off along a wide main road the following morning and made good progress until I called a halt after a mere two and a half hours. Moffat looked surprised and I explained my timing dilemma. His initial attitude was that we should get there as soon as possible, but I pointed out that he and Isiah also had to get back, so it behoved us to use the best method for all of us.

If that meant delays, so much the better provided we dallied in pleasant or interesting spots.

We made camp in a grove of huge trees only a few metres from the Zambezi but as the tents were being set up we were approached by a local villager. In shaky English he introduced himself as Tomas and asked us not to camp in that particular grove. It seemed that it was the village burial ground and he didn't want the Spirits disturbed.

He invited us to stay in his village which suited my companions, but I understood the reasoning behind the invitation and we duly went back to start again outside Tomas' hut.

His wife Lucaina welcomed us with a gentle curtsy and asked whether we wanted tea. Once again I was amazed, but accepted readily and gave her a load of Cowbell sachets for her pains.

Malula Village was spread out in chunks among fields of bananas and right behind Tomas' house was a small Catholic church –

another rarity in rural Mozambique.

With our tea, Lucaina produced a couple of delicious small bananas and I later bought forty of them off her for the equivalent of around twenty pence. Tomas assured me that Luabo was less than forty kilometres distant, so I knew I was well into the last hundred kilometres of my walk. That produced the usual ambivalent thinking. I wanted my walk to end but knew I would be sad and upset when we finally stopped.

A huge bush fire crackled through a nearby field of bananas that afternoon and the pall of black smoke must have been visible for kilometres around but nobody turned a hair. When I questioned Tomas about it and asked how much damage it would do to his bananas, he shrugged.

"Some will be lost," He told me. "Fires like that are difficult to stop, but they clear out the rubbish between the plants, so really they are good."

I vaguely saw his point.

Tomas had a son called George who had obviously never seen anyone like me. About eighteen months old, he followed me everywhere and when I sat on a borrowed chair outside my tent, George came waddling along and sat on the ground in front of me, staring up with wide brown eyes. I smiled at the little fellow and he smiled hesitantly back, so I spoke quietly to him. He obviously didn't understand a word, but when I filled my pipe and started puffing on it, I could see the astonishment in his eyes. A man lighting a fire inside his mouth so that he could blow smoke in the air was way beyond his comprehension and it showed.

I tried to explain it all to him and he gazed up at me with a rapt expression. I had emptied the tobacco tin and quietly called across to Tomas asking him if I could give the tin to George. He nodded with a smile and I held the tin out. Hesitantly a little hand came out to receive it and suddenly his face lit up with one of the biggest smiles I have seen.

I knew I had made a friend for life and for the rest of my stay in Malula, little George was at my heels, the round tin clutched firmly in his hand. When I sat, he sat and would play happily with that tin. He filled it with sand, shook it against his ear and emptied it again.

He filled it with stones and smiled at the little clatter when he shook it. He filled it with water and when Tomas finally sent him off to bed that evening, he was still holding his tin tightly to his chest. I found myself deeply moved that a gift I would normally have thrown away could cause such joy for one young man. My own grandchildren and every other child I knew in the 'civilised' world would have examined the tin, found it unappealing and discarded it, but to little George it was something to be treasured.

That evening, I wandered around the village and met up with the Secretary, Elsan Katundu who gently mocked my efforts at speaking Portuguese and addressed me in perfect English. He asked where I was going and shook my hand when I told him.

"You still have a long way to go My Friend," He said quietly. "But I pray that our Good Lord will keep you safe and allow you to succeed in your venture."

Shaking my hand again, he walked off into gathering darkness and I reflected that in this particular area of Mozambique, the missionaries had done their job. Mind you, the Catholicism seemed pretty localised. Two days previously, I had spotted a typewriter occupying centre stage in a village we passed through. Although ribbon less, it was spotlessly clean and mounted on a black tin box. I was assured by an Elder that this was the local Deity and a 'priest' had the onerous duty of polishing it every day. Part of a jet engine was similarly polished and kept clean in another village. It was obviously a remnant from the civil war, but the villagers were adamant in their belief that it had miraculously appeared in their midst one day.

Religion in Mozambique could be very confusing.

There was a brisk wind blowing intermittent drizzle into our faces when we left Tomas' village the following morning, but he insisted on guiding us for the first few kilometres. Taking advantage of distinctly cooler conditions we walked hard for five hours and made camp in a delightful spot overlooking the Zambezi. Suddenly I felt very content with life. I was nearly there and within a week should have achieved what no man had achieved before. That was a heady feeling and I found myself wallowing in a certain amount of self-congratulatory pride.

It was not to last. When I switched the pink and white phone on that evening, there were messages from Deborah and the German television bloke asking for an exact date for my arrival. I didn't know and replied immediately with that message. The phone rang and Mfanasibili Nkosi of ZDF told me that they wanted to film the whole of my arrival and would I mind if they spent the night before with me so that they could show my camp routine. Somewhat sourly I pointed out that I didn't know where I would end up or whether there were roads that would lead them to me. Nor did I know how I would get across to Chinde itself, as it was situated on an island in the mouth of the Zambezi.

Mfanasibili brushed my objections aside, but told me that they would have to hire a helicopter for aerial shots, so needed a date. All I could say was that I should be there in the first week of September but would know more when we reached Luabo which was the last major centre before Chinde. I promised to let him know when we were there but when I rang off, my initial euphoria had disappeared.

At no stage in the two hundred and eighty something days of walking had I had deadlines to meet. I could go where I wanted and when I wanted which was a major part of my walk. Modern man is seldom totally free and I revelled in having the freedom to choose my own path and timings. Now they were asking me to reach places at specified times and it just didn't seem right. This was my trip damnit and I would do it my way!

I was doubtless being unfair, but little worries and doubts were plaguing me at that stage. First Quantum would collect me from Chinde in due course, but what then? How would I survive once back in the modern world?

It was all somewhat upsetting, but all I could do was plod on the following day.

It was still August and officially winter which is the dry season south of the equator, but once again we were walking in the rain. In one village we passed through, two young women were pounding maize in the same pestle, singing in harmony and timing their blows to the rhythm of their song. It was a lovely sight and I should have taken a photograph, but didn't want to disturb them at their work.

In another village I laughed aloud as a little braided tot marched proudly along with a tiny clay pot balanced on her head. She was doubtless practicing for later life when she would carry water in larger vessels many times a day, but she was enjoying herself. Africa was exerting its charm again and my grumpiness subsided.

During the afternoon we found ourselves back on a road, whether by accident or design I wasn't sure, but I had to rely on my erstwhile guides. I didn't say anything and we suddenly found ourselves overwhelmed by a procession of Frelimo supporters dancing and singing their way along. As is the way with African political rallies, most of them were ululating women and one or two brandished placards quite ferociously in my face.

But we were close to the Zambezi again and having learned from our experience at Kondongo, I had Isiah ask around for the headman. I wanted to camp beside the water and had seen a beautifully shady grove of trees looking out across the river. The mosquitoes would doubtless be bad, but it was infinitely preferable to camping on the edge of a village.

At last we found him. Paulino Totot had a large house and a domineering wife called Beatrisia. She was the one who questioned us and she kept us hanging around for ages while she conferred with her husband, presumably as to our respectability. At last though, consent was given, Moffat bought a small brown hen from Beatrisia for supper and we made a nice, comfortable camp.

The mosquitoes were bad, but couldn't get at me in the tent although I could hear them whining against the gauze windows. My sleep was restless and disturbed, mainly because the prospect of looming 'normal' life was beginning to take over my thoughts.

In the morning I was scratchy-eyed and irritable but as we were packing up camp – I was drinking my tea – we had another visitor. Luigi Lota was a middle aged man who walked on a crutch as he only had one leg. He told us that he had lost it to a hippo many years ago, but still worked as a fisherman.

Only a few days previously we had chatted with a bloke who had lost an arm to a crocodile and he told a similar story, so I could only imagine the courage it took to resume their careers after such injuries. Luigi made me feel ashamed of my own troubled weakness and when we moved on, I was in a better frame of mind.

Again the weather was cool so we made excellent progress. I had told Mfanasibili that we would be in Luabo the next day so I pushed us hard. We reached the town during the afternoon and at the same time as the rain. This time, it wasn't cooling drizzle but an absolute downpour. Rain came down in heavy sheets of surprisingly cold water and within moments, all three of us were soaked to the skin. We took shelter for a while in a huge shed beside the river, but it was cold and the shed was full of other men sheltering from the rain. Acrid smoke from homemade cigarettes clogged the air and for once I lit my pipe, not for pleasure but in self-defence.

After half an hour of this I had had enough. We needed somewhere to sleep and not only was Luabo a fairly large town with its own run down port, but I had been told that it was right on the edge of the river delta. River deltas usually meant swampy conditions and the thought of camping like that with sodden clothing and equipment did not appeal.

Although the rain had eased, there was still a steady drizzle, but a bystander directed us to a small yellow building where he said they took in lodgers. It really was a tiny building and I was doubtful, but it had an annexe at the rear which comprised four small rooms in a straight line. We hired two of them but I did wonder whether we might have been better off camping in the rain.

It really was a fleapit, this one. Once again there were all the necessary fittings with taps, baths and cisterns but water had to be drawn from a garden well and wasn't overly clean. Our host warned us that the Luabo electricity supply came from a town generator which often ran out of diesel and he did not serve food. He smilingly added that he could fetch food for us from a nearby restaurant but sometimes it took a long time. We all ordered a meal – inevitably chicken and rice for me – and I added two beers and a couple of cokes each for the other two.

I wrote in my journal that evening, 'Hell this country is in a mess – even without the flies and mossies.' Sitting on the veranda – without electricity – I pondered on the dreadful state of what had once been a proud and very beautiful country. The Portuguese had been colonialists and probably hadn't treated the Mozambican people well, but once they fled the country, everything had been allowed to deteriorate until it was completely unworkable. Grand buildings were little more than ruins, some of them occupied, but the majority mere shells of what once had been. There was no piped water and electricity depended on the reliability of diesel supplies. Luabo was not a tiny forest village but a major river port and had once been a thriving town. It had a cathedral, a shopping centre, public statues and fine buildings. Now it was a desiccated husk of what once had been and my heart ached for the ordinary people of this country. I couldn't help wondering how they felt about freedom and independence now.

Having questioned a number of locals during the day, I determined that there was a path through the delta, but conditions were bad and the path ended at Nyakatiwa from where we could get a boat across to Chinde. It was less than sixty kilometres to Nyakatiwa, so I managed to contact Mfanasibili in Johannesburg and told him that we would be there on Thursday the fourth of September and in Chinde the following day. If he wanted to join us for the final night, he was welcome.

He asked if there was a road to Nyakatiwa, but I didn't think so. I felt that if they wanted to join us, they would probably have to hire a boat. Having promised to contact him again when we arrived in Nyakatiwa, I rang off and left them all to it. I didn't want to share my last night with anyone, but if they could get there I would have to put up with it, if only for the sake of my sponsors. After all, Cowbell would get some good publicity out of it.

I was still a very confused and anxious man when I retired to bed that night – after checking my room for cockroaches and other unwanted creepy crawlies.

CHAPTER SEVENTEEN
(Mud Mangroves and Mosquitoes)

We left Luabo through what had obviously been an upmarket suburb in days gone by. Huge old houses of grand design scowled on our passing through glassless windows and most doors had obviously been taken for firewood. Yards were overgrown with weeds and I reflected that during my months of walking through the country, I hadn't seen more than a dozen lawns. Those had been at kapenta camps on the lake, the police station at Nyakoro and the lodges at Casindira and Mphingwe. Margi Carlisle had built a beautiful garden with rolling lawns on Manyerere Island, but the only other grass I had seen during my travels had been of the wild, brown, bush variety.

Margi and the others mentioned above had grown flowers in their gardens, but apart from them the only blooms I had seen had been deep in the bush where they were growing wild. Somehow a country without flowers seems to have something missing – a touch of character perhaps. I wished I had seen this and similar towns in the Portuguese era and wondered whether there would have been lawns and gardens then.

A vast building loomed up on the edge of town and we stopped to look at it. Once again it had been reduced to a shell and a faded notice told me that it had once been a sugar refinery. How many workers must have lost their livelihoods when the management moved out and how many lives had been ruined by their loss. It was all so sad and I contrasted the ruined building with the factories still managing to run in my own Zimbabwe. Africa has a habit of biting itself in the foot and I am sure colonialism can't be blamed for everything.

Shrugging my gloomy thoughts away, I started walking once more. I had a job to finish and it wasn't done yet.

Among all the abandoned mansions, there was one with a fairly new looking vehicle outside and curtains at the windows. As we approached, we were intercepted by a thick set fellow who told us that the governor wanted to see us. Leaving our packs on the ground, we walked across to the occupied building where Governor

Oswaldo came out to greet us.

A charming man, he was dressed in an expensive looking charcoal suit, shiny black shoes and a bright scarlet Frelimo tee shirt. He listened attentively when I told him what we were doing and frowned when I told him where we were going.

"It is not safe in the delta," He said in reasonable English. "It is very wet and many people die. Be careful My Friend. I have heard about your walk and do not want it to end badly in my area."

But he gave us his blessing and asked me to send his felicitations to Governor Camera of Chinde. This I promised to do and once again, we were on the road.

It started raining again as we left the town, but we were soon deep in a forest so it didn't matter too much. Tall trees absorbed the rain and we remained relatively dry. The going was awful though. The path we followed was horribly wet and slippery. I fell a couple of times so that I was soon very muddy and to my surprise, Isiah, long the strongest of us also went down on one occasion. Somehow I didn't feel we were going to get very far that day and wondered whether the estimated time of arrival I had given Mfanasibili might have been too optimistic.

Governor Oswaldo had told me that we were about forty-five kilometres from Nyakatiwa, so we might take four days rather than my estimated three, but I told myself it didn't matter. This was still my walk and if the TV blokes had to wait for me, that was not my problem.

Once we became accustomed to the slippery conditions our pace picked up a little and by noon, we had covered a good ten kilometres, so I settled down to walk for another couple of hours before finding somewhere to camp.

The only problem with that was the lack of anywhere suitable. The Zambezi was a few hundred metres away to our right, but whenever we took a look at it, the banks were sheer and fields of sweet potatoes and millet ran right up to the edge. There were few trees, the atmosphere was horribly steamy and each of us walked in the centre of a mosquito cloud. I could feel the little pests biting my neck and visions of more malaria began to cloud my judgement. Thus it was – I think – that I chose the worst and most uncomfortable spot we had camped in throughout our journey.

It was on the edge of a field full of sorghum, had one tree for shelter from the rain and was surrounded by thick, gooey mud. There was no firewood on hand and we were all soon covered in muck.

But we were committed or so I told myself. The tents went up and Moffat went down to the river for water. Isiah managed to find a few damp branches and with true African ingenuity, he soon had a smoky fire going. We had little to eat, but I still had a few sticks of mouldy biltong, so I shared them out and we chewed morosely.

Still it rained. Halfway through the afternoon we had another deluge and I almost longed to be back in our Luabo fleapit. I could remember watching footage of Ed Stafford striding toward the finish of his epic Amazon walk. He walked along a wide road, his companion beside him and a posse of photographers following them. Stafford and his South American Indian companion completed an incredible number of kilometres – I think it was eighty odd – during their last twenty-four hours and I marvelled at the strength of the man. He had already walked a far greater distance than I had on the Zambezi and was still going strong, while I was slipping and stumbling my way along, barely able to cover twelve kilometres in a day.

I consoled myself with the fact that he was considerably younger than I was and I had always shunned publicity in any case. The German crew might make the finish, but apart from Mfanasibili, Deborah and a couple of folk in Zambia, nobody knew where I was.

Thoughts of Stafford and his guide led me to think about my own guides. In fact, they were more porters and helpers than guides, but like Stafford with his bloke, I had grown close to them over the weeks. Despite occasionally losing my temper and a few sulky spats on their part, I think we enjoyed mutual admiration for each other and had formed an excellent little team. They had certainly made my life considerably easier and probably cut a few months off my journey time, but it was more than that. When my spirits were really down, Moffat's cheery good humour made me feel better and although Isiah's high pitched laugh could be extremely irritating, it was also very infectious and I couldn't be cross for long.

When the rain finally stopped, I managed to get to the river bank and sat for a while, just watching the Mighty Zambezi. It was wide and muddy at this point, little white ripples studding its surface. For a moment I thought I was losing my marbles. The river was often rippled as the wind pushed the flow along, but these ripples were going upstream. That surely couldn't be right and I called Moffat across to bear me out.

He too looked utterly bewildered when he realised what I was getting at.

"The river is going the wrong way Boss," He commented. "Perhaps the Zambezi wants to go home."

It took me a while to work it out, but we were close to the sea and the incoming tide was pushing against the current and causing the ripples. It looked very strange and climbing down to the edge of the water, I had a taste and it was brackish and horrible. I couldn't help wondering how local villagers coped.

There were compensations for them though. The damp, sultry conditions of the swamp – for swamp it definitely was – were obviously perfect for growing things. Sweet potatoes grew profusely in the field beside our camp, but there were also coconut palms, bananas and paw paws, all of them looking healthy and productive. We had walked past crops of millet, sorghum and maize so the local people obviously had an excellently healthy diet to keep them going.

For all that, although population seemed sparse I had never seen an area with so many graves. It seemed that every twenty metres or so along the track, we were passing one or two simple headstones and earlier in the day I had asked a villager what all these people had died from.

"Malaria." Was his succinct reply and I felt a shiver up my spine.

When I switched the pink and white on that evening, there was another message from Mfanasibili, telling me he would meet me at Nyakatiwa on Saturday morning. That was all very well, but it would mean waiting for him and I was not prepared to wait very long. I couldn't get through to him, but messaged Deborah who was also in contact with the TV people and asked her to tell them that if they weren't there as promised, I would move on to Chinde. I didn't feel it was fair that I should have to tailor my movements around them at this stage of the walk.

When I put the phone away, I noticed that Moffat and Isiah were arguing. This was a rare occurrence and I asked Moffat whet the trouble was.

"Zaire says that the boat to Chinde leaves from the other side at Chacuma, not from Nyakatiwa," He explained and I was aghast. Chacuma was on the southern bank of the river and it would mean either taking a dug out – and we hadn't seen many of those – across or walking back to Luabo and hiring a boat to start again on the southern bank.

"What do you think?" I asked Moffat and he frowned.

"I think he is wrong," Was his verdict. 'Even the governor in Luabo told us to head for Nyakatiwa. We must go on because as you keep saying, we can't go back."

So it was decided, but Isiah sulked through that evening and my mind was in turmoil as I wondered who was correct. How I wished I had learned Portuguese properly before venturing into Mozambique. At least then I could have heard for myself rather than relying on my companions to translate things. It was a weird set up, inasmuch that Isiah would hold the conversation in whatever local language there was. He would then relay the exchange to Moffat in chiShona and Moffat would tell me in English. Inevitably there had to be slip ups and I wondered if this was one of them.

I didn't sleep well that night, but we were on the road again early the next day. With the disagreement of the previous evening, I was in a hurry because if we had to go all the way back to Luabo, it would add another three or four days to our trip and I did not want that.

This should have been the most enjoyable part of my entire walk, but with the rain, the conditions underfoot and so many other factions suddenly involved, it was becoming a nightmare.

* * *

There were few people about as we plodded on through gentle drizzle but the state of the path we were following deteriorated rapidly. At each step, my Courtney boots submerged themselves in mud and each such soggy sinking brought another cloud of mosquitoes to harry and hassle us. Moffat reckoned that it was like walking through bees because they made so much noise. Wet clothes stuck to our bodies and even Isiah retreated into his thoughts.

Uncomfortable step followed uncomfortable step and I suppose we made progress but it was hardly fast. But there certainly wasn't any hurry now. It was only Wednesday and if we had to wait until Saturday in this horrible swamp, it was not going to be pleasant.

We had another uncomfortable camp although we had bought mealies and green coconuts from a roadside hut, so we ate well and went to bed, damp but replete. I contacted Andy Taylor during the evening and told him that we would arrive in Chinde over the weekend. He promised to liaise with First Quantum Minerals about the flight, but got hold of me the following day to say that the mine aircraft was being serviced, so we couldn't be collected till the following Saturday. I relayed this to my companions and a pall of gloom descended on our party. We seemed to be waiting on everyone else when we had so nearly done what we had set out to do.

Once again we were out early and making slow progress to Nyakatiwa. We passed another flurry of grave stones and again were told by locals that the occupants had succumbed to malaria. We were all being badly bitten by the horrible little pests, but there was nothing we could do about that. The one relief came when a local confirmed that there was a regular boat to Chinde from Nyakatiwa. I felt like glaring at Isiah for the worry he had caused me but we were so close to the finish that magnanimity took over.

It was late morning and the rain had eased when the path seemed to widen out, turned a corner and moved straight down to the river. A small banca looked down on the water and we went in there for a coke.

"Nyakatiwa?" I queried and the storekeeper nodded his head.

"Nyakatiwa."

I had done it. I had walked the Zambezi from source to sea and become the first person to do so. We couldn't see the ocean yet, but I could hear the thunder of surf through the trees. The island of Chinde was in front of us and all we had to do was cross the water and walk through the town.

I wasn't sure how I felt, but we still had to wait for the television people.

We had passed what looked like an abandoned school beside a football field a couple of kilometres before Nyakatiwa, It had looked like a good place to camp as there were tall trees around the ramshackle building, so back we walked and commenced what promised to be a long vigil. It was Thursday the fourth of September and it seemed unbelievable that I had no more walking to do. All the difficulties and troubles of my ten-month journey were behind me. All I had to do now was survive the mosquitoes and the rain for a couple of days, then it really would be all over.

It was a heady feeling and I went to bed that evening feeling quite pleased with myself.

CHAPTER EIGHTEEN
(Journey's End)

There is something soothing about rain on the roof when one is tucked up in bed and I smiled to myself as I woke to the pitter patter of drops on the roof of my tent. Moffat and Isiah had set up their quarters in the old schoolhouse, but my tent was out in the open beneath a tall tree. It had been a lovely position in daylight, but I had yet again been foolish in not following the example of the other two.

I went back to sleep after the rain started but was woken again shortly after midnight. This time it was a large drop of water that woke me by splashing on to my face. The rain was considerably harder than it had been initially and wind was tearing at the tent. I knew my body weight would hold it down, but in the light of my torch I could see water running freely down the walls of my little shelter. It was on the inside too and my blanket was already very wet.

I had most of my kit, including precious notebooks on the floor beside my bed and hurried to get them away from the incoming rain. I was tempted to yell for Moffat and have the tent moved, but the rain outside was torrential and in those conditions, it would have been almost impossible to get it done. A pool was forming in the middle of the floor and I pushed myself against one wall to try and keep as much of my bedding dry as possible. That was another mistake as I could feel moisture seeping through the flimsy fabric and soaking into my back.

Gloomily I wondered what to do. I had slept in awful conditions many times in the past, but on this trip it was the first time I had been totally soaked through during the night. Curling myself into a miserable ball, I endured the discomfort and waited miserably for daylight. Hour after hour went by and if anything, the thunder of the storm outside increased in volume. Water continued to run down the walls, drop from the roof and pool on the floor so sleep was impossible. Grimly I prayed for the storm to blow over, but this time, God was not on my side.

The irony of my situation was not lost on me either. A few hours previously I had been feeling pleased with myself and looking forward to a comfortable night, now I was feeling more miserable and uncomfortable than I had over the previous months of walking. Chinde and the end of the road were almost within touching distance, yet I was curled up in a damp ball of discomfort just wishing the hours away. Quietly and monotonously I called curses into the night. I cursed the rain, I cursed the mosquitoes, I cursed that awful swamp of the Zambezi Delta. Most of all, I cursed myself, firstly for camping out in the open when I would have been better off in the rickety schoolhouse and secondly for thinking I could walk the Zambezi in the first place. At my advanced age, I should surely have known better.

I tried to lose myself in pleasant memories of the wonders I had seen and the fantastic people I had met along the way, but wrapped up in wet bedding and sodden clothing as I was, it was difficult to think of anything but my own miseries.

Hour after hour crawled by. Water continued to accumulate around me and my discomfort and melancholy increased by the moment. When at last daylight slowly filtered in to my soggy abode, I crawled out of the tent and yelled for Moffat and Isiah.

With the coming of daylight, the rain had eased to a steady drizzle and my two cut throats emerged bleary-eyed and tousled from their dry if somewhat claustrophobic shelter. I explained my predicament, showed them the wreckage of my tent and the three of us carted my sodden belongings into the old schoolhouse. Irritably I demanded that a fire be made for tea, but even that was a long slow process. Lost in the euphoria of success, none of us had thought to collect firewood the previous day and what there was around the camp was absolutely soaked.

Townie though he undoubtedly was, Isiah performed a miracle of the arsonist's art and eventually managed to coax small, smoky flames from the wet wood and my first task was to try and warm myself up. We had bought sugar at the Nyakatiwa banca and when it finally arrived, my tea was heavily sweetened. Moffat wandered off to the nearby village to see how we could dry everything off, while Isiah and I huddled together in the smoky confines of the schoolhouse.

The rain had finally died away when Moffat returned with the local headman whose name was Vita and who spoke both French and Swahili. I still had vestiges of my schoolboy French and my Swahili wasn't bad, so at least we could talk.

Vita had brought a number of villagers with him, some carrying firewood and others with green mealies or coconuts. Our sorry little fire was soon blazing brightly and at last I could feel the chill easing from my body. This wonderful man then took my bedding and a saturated shirt away with him for drying and I marvelled yet again at the generosity of these simple villagers. It had been the same throughout my two hundred and ninety days on the road and I reflected that whatever else my Zambezi Walk had taught me, it had certainly changed my always jaundiced view of people.

The area around the schoolhouse had been transformed into a vast pool of water and my grim mood lightened slightly when I noticed a duck swimming across, followed by five tiny ducklings. At least someone had benefitted from the deluge.

There wasn't much else to cheer me up though but later in the morning, we received another visitor, this time Governor Camera himself. He shook my hand and told me that he would be away from Chinde when I arrived, but he had told his Town Clerk to ensure that I was treated well. That was a nice gesture from an important man.

The pink and white had also suffered from the rain and as my Power Monkey had little life in it and there was no sun to charge it, I sent my phone down to the banca for charging. When it came back a couple of hours later, I sat down to see exactly what the situation was and how long we had to wait for the television crew. Mfanasibili told me that he would have his boss ring me and not long afterward, Timm Kroeger came through to say that a camera had broken down and he would fly in to Chinde as soon as he could with a spare. That was all very well, but it would mean further delay and I dreaded another two or three days in the claustrophobic schoolhouse, particularly if we had more rain.

Feeling very disgruntled, I sent a message to Deborah, telling her what had happened and reiterating that I would wait until the next day and if the crew hadn't arrived, I would move on to Chinde and to hell with television coverage.

My Daughter knows my impatient nature only too well and urged me to keep my temper in check and just 'go with the flow.'

"It is for your good, Dad," Were her words and the message made me smile. I didn't really want publicity of any sort, but felt somewhat flattered that a television company regarded my arrival in Chinde as newsworthy.

Another message that cheered me up was the usual 'Go Madala Go' from Rasta Alexis in Lusaka and I replied with the news that I didn't need to 'go' any longer as I was almost there.

Apart from the flurry of phone messages and calls, the day was long and damp. Vita proved an absolute star and we had a succession of visitors arrive with gifts of fruit to keep us going. An Elder called Saturday (he looked even older than me) wanted his photograph taken, so I posed with him and he was delighted to see his own image on the back of the camera. Isiah went off to play football, Moffat went off to do whatever Moffat had to do and I spent much of the day walking slowly around the football field, not only to warm myself up, but to try and make sense of the turmoil in my mind.

Everybody was making such a fuss of me and I ought to have been feeling ten foot tall, but inside I felt flat and dispirited. The future frightened me and I wasn't sure how I would fare back in the real world. I had spent nearly a year as a scruffy vagabond without plans, now I would be back to routine and responsibilities.

It was difficult to get my mind around the situation, but I still had to reach Chinde. The town on the island was regarded as the true end or beginning of any Zambezi adventure, but I wasn't there yet and my impatience mounted by the moment.

Late in the afternoon, my bedding and bush shirt were returned by Vita. Everything was dry and somehow ironed and I gave him fish hooks and needles in grateful exchange. What a good man he was proving to be. In that he was so typical of the Zambezi River People and I knew in my heart that without folk like this little headman, I would not have completed my foolish adventure. Throughout my days on the road, they had helped me, cosseted me and picked me up when I was down. From lordly chiefs to ordinary fishermen, with hoteliers, missionaries and others in between, I had met only nice people.

I suppose in a way it was a salutary lesson to me that my cynical views on humanity were not always correct.

My mood soured again that evening when Timm Kroeger who had asked me to keep my phone switched on, came through again with the news that his crew wouldn't reach me until Sunday as they had encountered more problems with the helicopter. I think he must have been in contact with Deborah as he was very conciliatory and apologetic. Fortunately perhaps, the rain had stopped and my tent was now in the derelict schoolroom, so I agreed to wait another day. From the sound of his voice, Timm was expecting more of an argument from me – which is why I am sure he had been speaking to Deborah – and before ringing off, he assured me that the team would be in Nyakatiwa at eleven o'clock on Sunday morning.

I told him that we would be waiting and wondered if the deadline would change yet again.

Saturday was another boring day, enlivened a little by a display of coconut collecting from a mite called January. He could not have been more than six years old, but he shinned a good eight metres up the tree using only his hands and feet. Once in the foliage, he dislodged green coconuts and threw them down to us. I marvelled at his dexterity but the green coconuts were truly delicious and made me realise what we miss in so-called civilisation. Even in African towns, coconuts, although nutritious and nice to eat are pretty dry once the milk has gone. When they are green, the milk seems sweeter and the flesh is deliciously tender. They were small, but January's father presented us each with a pile of the fruit and we gorged ourselves for an hour or two.

At last it was evening and I told Moffat and Isiah that we would dismantle and pack up the camp the following morning and be at the jetty for eleven o'clock. If the television people hadn't arrived by two thirty, we would take a local craft across to Chinde and to hell with the loss of publicity. They seemed quite agreeable with that as I think they were as bored as I was. The people of Nyakatiwa were lovely, but their village was very basic, there was nothing for any of us to do and the mosquitoes were truly appalling, even during the day.

Eleven o'clock on Sunday found the three of us sitting on a log outside the banca, looking out across the wide and muddy Zambezi.

There was quite a bit of traffic and I amused myself by watching what were obviously local buses, piled to the gunwales with people, livestock and bicycles. As one puttered ashore, a motor cyclist raced down to the water and there followed a hectic ten minutes as assorted passengers struggled to swing the heavy machine inboard.

It was all very colourful, noisy and typically African. How I was going to miss it.

One o'clock found the three of us still sitting on our log, but chewing sweet biscuits and drinking the horribly sugary Mozambican fizzy drinks. I was very bored although both my companions occupied themselves with chatting to local women washing pots in the river, then stretched out on the ground and went to sleep. I envied them their ability to switch off in the most trying of circumstances.

It was getting close to two o'clock when my phone rang. It was Mfanasibili to say that they were about to board a boat at Chacuma and would be with us in forty minutes. I didn't mention that they had almost missed my deadline, but did wonder what had happened to the aircraft and why they were leaving from Chacuma rather than Chinde.

Still, that was not my problem and I prodded the blokes awake and told them the news. Then I went for a solitary walk inland. Mud was still thick on the ground and mosquitoes still swarmed around my face, but I felt a sudden sense of deep regret that I was leaving it all behind. Despite the terrible conditions we had endured over the past five or six days, they had provided me with a surfeit of memories and making memories is surely what life is all about. I didn't suppose many men had walked through that terribly hostile environment and as it was, I had only survived it because I was carrying a lighter pack than the others and through the kindness of people along the way.

Back on the log, I was in a sombre state of mind as I watched a trim looking speed boat cream through the water toward us. A white man in the front waved and the three of us moved down to the water.

Timm Kroeger – I had met him in Johannesburg – was first out of the boat and he was followed by Mfanasibili and a big cameraman called Joe. Handshakes and congratulations followed and I was

182

about to swing my pack on to the boat, when Timm asked if we could do some filming.

Back up the track we went and then we pantomimed walking through the bush with Joe walking backward in front of us. We used the track for a couple of takes and then went into the scrub to make it seem as though we were walking through real jungle. As usual, mosquitoes had a lot of fun around us and not for the first time, I wondered how much of what one sees presented as fact on television is carefully posed and rehearsed.

At last it was over and we climbed aboard the boat. Moffat and Isiah sat on the stern and I sat beside Timm so that he could interview me as we went. That meant the boat had to slow right down so that engine noise didn't drown our voices and I could feel myself chafing at the delay. My walk was effectively over but I would not be able to say that I had completed it until we had gone through Chinde to the sea on the other side of town.

At four fifteen precisely on Sunday the seventh of September in the year two thousand and fourteen, the prow of the boat bit into the sand at Chinde harbour and I was there. After two hundred and ninety-two days, spread over three years, I had become the first person in recorded history to walk from the source of the Zambezi in the corner of north western Zambia through to the Indian ocean at Chinde in Mozambique. In the course of the journey I had covered three thousand two hundred and a few kilometres and it had all been great fun – to look back on at any rate.

As I jumped ashore, my pink and white buzzed in my pocket. It was a message from Deborah and it read as follows, 'Dad are you there yet? Hundreds of people are waiting to hear whether you have arrived. Please let me know so that I can pass the word.'

I could feel a lump in my throat but messaged back to explain that I had just arrived so could she text me again in ten minutes or so.

She did better than that. Exactly ten minutes later, I was walking along the main street in Chinde with Moffat on one side and Isiah on the other. Joe was backing away in front of us and a huge lens was pointing into my face when the pink and white actually rang.

It was Deborah again and as soon as I heard her voice, I burst into tears. So did she and I gulpingly accepted her congratulations, told her I loved her – that brought more floods of tears – and asked her to phone again the following day, by which time we would be better able to speak to each other.

As I put the phone away, Joe grinned at me around the camera.

"That was great television," He told me. "I have it all on camera."

It was only then that I realised I was festooned with microphones, so every word and every tear had been recorded.

"Don't you dare use that bit," I said darkly. "That was a private moment between me and my daughter and it would not be good for my reputation."

When I watched the documentary a few months later, they had given me over four minutes out of forty, so that was pretty generous. Unfortunately the commentary was in German, but thankfully, they didn't use my tearful conversation with Deborah. I was supposed to be a hard man damnit! What would that have done to my credibility?

But we weren't finished. The light was fading fast and rather than film the beach scenes that evening, it was decided to leave it till the morning. The TV crew had booked into a local rest house and took us there. After checking on prices, I booked us in as well and we settled down to a night of merriment and good cheer. Timm bought dinner for everyone and I dined on fat Mozambique prawns, washed down with 'Lord Gin' and tonic. The gin didn't taste much like the western versions, but I didn't care. This was my evening and I was going to enjoy it.

I was up early the following morning but nobody else seemed in any hurry to get going. I wandered the streets of Chinde, once again seeing beautiful old buildings that had been allowed to decay. The streets themselves were wide and straight, so the town had obviously been a great place in its heyday. An ornate old prison was falling down, its turreted battlements standing tall among heaps of rubble.

For the first time in a while, the weather was nice and the sun was warm on my back. Walking briskly back to the fleapit, I tried to hurry everybody up. My Zambezi Walk had officially ended, but there was one thing I still had to do.

I still had to put a foot in the sea. Once that was done, I could finally relax and know that I really had achieved what I set out to achieve almost three years previously.

Back in Nyakatiwa, Vita had warned me not to walk in Chinde without shoes. He said there was a little *skelm* living in the sands and that it liked to crawl into feet and was very painful. That Monday morning I forgot all about his warning. We walked briskly along the sand and I breathed deeply of the sea air, savouring the moment. Once again, Joe walked backward in front of me while Timm walked quietly at my side. I think he realised the emotion I was feeling and although I had promised him another interview, he knew it would have to come later.

There were few people on that glorious beach and I was thankful for that. One group of fishermen hauled a long wooden boat through the shallows and a party of women carried firewood on their heads. All of them looked at our little party in some surprise, but I think it was more the sight of Joe's big camera and peculiar gait that startled them, rather than seeing two white faces amongst us.

Nobody seemed in any hurry and I didn't want to make a fool of myself by rushing toward the water. That would have been too undignified and I sensed that the others were waiting for me to make the first move, so I plodded slowly on, trying to look as though this was just another day.

I think it was Moffat who broke the spell. Suddenly, we rounded a corner and there in front of us were rolling breakers pounding in on the sand. My two lovely cut throats immediately started to run, but Timm called them back. For the television, I had to go first and I suppose it was only fitting.

Forgetting all about Vita's warning, I took my boots and socks off, propped my walking pole against then and walked with measured tread into the Indian Ocean. It felt cool and rather wonderful so I burst into tears.

Now it really was all over. I still needed to get back to Zambia, but my walk was finished. With a big smile on his face, Timm walked across to me, shook my hand and started a rather sniffly – on my part at any rate – interview. Half way through, we were interrupted by excited shrieks and yells from the water and Joe swung the camera off me.

Although they lived beside one of the largest man-made lakes in the world, Moffat and Isiah had never seen the sea. As soon as they were able to, they had stripped off their clothes and were frolicking among the waves like excited children. It was heart-warming to watch and my tears were momentarily forgotten.

The two of them had been with me and supported me for many weeks and together we had walked four hundred and fifty odd kilometres. It had been hard and sometimes difficult. On occasion, they had driven me to distraction with their antics and on other occasions, I had snapped and snarled at them without any particular justification for my irritation. Both of them had been sulky at times, but they had always done what I asked them to do and together, the three of us had made a pretty good team.

Now they were enjoying a brand new experience and I smiled indulgently at their shrieks of laughter.

Before Moffat and Isiah came along, I had only had company on two occasions. With Mawaya and Ronnie, they had been part of our squad on the Livingstone Trail and before that Martin and James had escorted me down the wild Kalomo river in Zambia. In spite of my well known antipathy to company on my adventures, they had all made huge contributions to the success of this one.

I had a paddle myself and went in deep enough for the sea to wet my shorts, but wasn't going to swim. I was still very emotional and for a while I wandered away from the others and just sat on the sand, staring out to sea. Eventually I wandered back, we met up with Mfanasibili who had taken the crew's hired truck into a village and then drove back to the rest house. They were leaving after lunch, but we still had five days to wait in Chinde, so I felt we deserved another night of relative comfort.

Just before the film crew moved out, Timm approached me with a frown on his face and warned me to be careful when settling the bill. He told me that the landlady, Shina after who the Shinita rest house was named had done her best to charge him a lot more than he owed. She had also tried to insist that he paid for our stay as well.

"Be careful she doesn't try to charge you for us," He went on. "The dinner last night was on me, but I have a feeling that she will try to make you pay for that as well."

I promised to be careful and after handshakes all round, they drove off into the afternoon, leaving us to our own devices. The first thing we had to do was check out the airstrip which was a kilometre or so out of town and I cursed myself for not going out there with the film crew. It would have saved us a walk and I felt we had done enough of that for the moment.

It was an easy walk along a long, dusty road, but when we reached the strip I was horrified. Waist high bushes and even a dozen or so sturdy saplings all but covered the runway and this would have to be cleared before the First Quantum aeroplane arrived.

Back we went to the governor's office, but Governor Camera had already told me he would be away in Quelimane, so I asked for the Secretary. He was away for the day and so was the 'second secretary.' A helpful young man called Frank promised to inform the secretary about the problem and told me I should return in the morning, so I had to make do with that.

I asked Frank if there was any place to camp in the town and he took us what must have once been a beautiful football stadium. Now the stand was falling down and weeds grew up through the concrete seating. Next door was the shell of an old theatre and I prowled through it but like most public buildings in Mozambique, it was also little more than a ruin. Nevertheless there was ample room on the football ground and the grass would be soft underfoot.

That night, there was no electricity in the rest house, so I sat quietly in the dining room and eventually started chatting with a portly gentleman wearing a very smart suit. He was drinking red wine which looked much nicer than my tepid beer, so when he offered me a glass, I accepted with alacrity.

Carlos Jessen turned out to be a former Minister of Finance in the Frelimo government. He was a Chinde boy and with a general election approaching had come home to campaign for Frelimo. He was also excellent company and had been all over the world, so we had an interesting conversation. Another bottle of red was produced and when I asked him why he had such an unAfrican name, he laughed and told me about his grandfather.

The original Jessen, had come out from Denmark in nineteen fourteen, married a local girl and produced nine children.

"Each of them went on to produce seven or eight kids," Carlos laughed, "so there are a large number of Jessens around the world. My grandmother's mother was a Coetzee, so that adds even more to the family mix.

'Mind you, Grandpa Jessen must have been a brave man, because to marry a nigger girl in that era would have been very much frowned upon."

It proved to be a lovely evening and I went to bed feeling that my Zambezi Walk had ended well.

* * *

The following day started well and ended badly. Our first call was at the Governor's office, which was in a huge building on the edge of town. Outwardly magnificent, it was dirty and unpainted inside. We managed to see the Town Secretary and I asked him if he would please clean up the airstrip so that First Quantum could get in on Saturday.

He hummed and ha'd a bit before asking whether I was prepared to pay for a team of workers who would clear the strip. I most certainly was not and told him so.

"We have very few aeroplanes visiting Chinde," He leaned back in an ornately carved chair and contemplated me over his spectacles. I don't think he was reassured by my somewhat unkempt appearance. I had bathed that morning and Moffat had washed my clothes the previous night, but my shirt was torn and hung loosely around my middle, while my shorts had repeatedly suffered tiny burns from sparks emanating from my pipe.

"You have seen the airfield?" He asked and I nodded.

"Then you will know it will be an expensive exercise to clear it. We shall need at least two hundred people and it will take three days or more."

"All the more reason for hurry," I pointed out. "The overseas press will be here in force when that aircraft arrives and you don't want them to get a bad impression of your town.

'Besides, Governor Camera promised me in his absence, that I could call on you if ever I needed anything."

I think it was mention of the governor rather than my empty threat about the overseas press that swung the argument because suddenly the secretary was all smiles. He promised to enlist the necessary two hundred and fifty – I had thought twenty would be more than sufficient – and have them start work the following day. That certainly took a load off my mind.

Chinde had a museum, a library and a Maritime Centre, but the first two were a desperate disappointment. The library contained some lovely old books in Portuguese, some of them dating back a hundred and fifty years, but they were all mouldy and some were completely waterlogged. The librarian if such he was, merely shrugged when I pointed out the damage.

"No cash," Was his comment and I supposed he was right, but left the building feeling sad at the waste of it all.

The museum was even worse. Sections of ceiling had fallen in and what few pitiful exhibits there were must have been wet through whenever it rained.

Ruefully I remembered Carlos Jessen's stories the previous evening. He had told me bits about the history of Chinde – and a fascinating history it was – and mused that it ought to be preserved for future generations. It seemed that nobody agreed with him.

Ronnie Henwood had told me that the Maritime Centre at Chinde was well worth a visit and held log books that went back a long way.

"Every incoming and outgoing boat has been recorded through the ages," Ronnie had been full of enthusiasm. "You can spend hours there if you are interested."

I was certainly interested but nobody in the centre knew what had happened to the log books. The Assistant Commodore whose name was Cassado looked smart in a very nautical uniform and his English was good. He could tell us little about the history of Chinde however and I left the building feeling extremely disappointed. It was a fascinating town and many great navigators and explorers must have visited over the centuries, yet nobody seemed to care. Livingstone must have been here on occasions too and I resolved to ask Ronnie about that when we met up again.

Back at the rest house, I asked for the bill and nearly had a heart attack when it came. Although it was itemised, everything was in Portuguese and nobody could translate for me. The figures were in the universal language though and totted up to over eight thousand meticais – a cool two hundred and sixty dollars.

"For two nights here?" I could feel my temper rising. "We could have stayed in a proper hotel for that."

"There are no hotels in Chinde," Shina seemed to have suddenly learned a bit of English. "So you stay here."

I sent Moffat to look for Carlos Jessen my friend of the previous evening but he was not to be seen and I remembered him telling me that he would be out campaigning for the day.

With the help of Moffat and Isiah, I pored through that ruddy receipt and soon realised that Timm's warning had been right on the nail. I was being charged for our initial dinner – something that he had already paid. I roared my indignation at this but Shina continued to look smug.

"You pay," She kept saying and a villainous looking henchman suddenly appeared from an inner sanctum. I wondered how many more might be in there, but was too cross to worry about it. The police station was a few hundred metres away, so I got everyone together and went there for some arbitration.

I had heard a number of horror stories about the police in Mozambique and that worried me a little. People told of being stopped at road blocks and having to pay bribes in order that their vehicles were not impounded for no reason at all. Others bemoaned the fact that officialdom of all branches seemed to make up rules and regulation as they went along. I had met few ordinary Mozambican coppers since entering the country, but most of them – with the exception of the ultra-suspicious Lorenzo at Nyakoro - had been friendly and interested in what I was doing.

That was about to change. The first shock to my system came when Shina was greeted with a hug and a torrent of friendly words from the sergeant on duty. She pointed at me and let loose a flood of what was obviously invective even though I couldn't understand a word. Nor could my companions and Moffat urged me to just pay the money and get out of there. Unfortunately I have a horror of being taken for a ride and my dander was up.

We were taken through to a side office where a more senior man sat behind a desk. He too greeted Shina with obvious enthusiasm and my spirits drooped even further. Beside me, Moffat was visibly trembling and there were tears in his eyes when he looked at me.

"They will lock us up and nobody will ever know," He murmured plaintively. "Pay the money Boss and let's go before something bad happens."

I turned to the senior officer and tried to put my case, but he imperiously waved me to silence. When Shina had told her story yet again – I hadn't been asked for mine – he looked at me, held out his hand and said one word.

"Passport."

I asked why and in hesitant but understandable English, he told me that he would lock it away and I could have it back when I had paid the bill.

I was really angry now and told him in the most basic English I could dig out of my mind that he was the most corrupt policeman I had ever come across and a disgrace to his uniform. I asked for his name and number, but the hand was still held out in my direction.

"Passport."

I was beaten and I knew it. Wearily I took my wallet out and handed a wad of notes to Shina. Her eyes gleamed as she carefully counted it into her henchman's hands and after a final glare at the smug looking policeman, I led my little party outside and into the football stadium.

It was an ignominious moment and I felt ashamed of myself for giving in to blatant dishonesty, but in the circumstances, there wasn't much else we could do.

We slept on the football field, but the following day we moved out to the airstrip. When we reached the place, I was amazed to see at least three hundred people lined up and being selected for work by a uniformed official. The clamour was appalling, but eventually two hundred and fifty were chosen to do the job and those turned away moved disconsolately back to town.

I told the official that we needed at least a thousand metres of runway and he readily agreed to organise this. Leaving him to it, we wandered into nearby villages in search of a place to set up camp for the last few days.

Our final camp was set up in Faina Village where the little tents went up beneath shady mango trees and we received a grand welcome from Zeka Jose and his family. Zeka's brother Adriano was instructed to look after us and they all made us feel instantly at home with fresh coconuts and big smiles from everyone. Zeka's wife Irena produced ncima and fish for lunch and we sat around on plastic chairs to eat. Joaquina, a matronly woman who was either Irena's sister or her friend marched up to me, gave me a hug and planted a kiss on each of my cheeks. I felt myself blushing and had the sudden thought that this would be my last hero's welcome for a while.

Our last three days were peaceful but traumatic at the same time. Every few hours I would wander down to the airstrip to check on progress, but while everyone worked hard the first day and cleared about half the required distance, Thursday afternoon saw the majority of workers take off for political meetings in town.

The following morning there was a strike. The governor's officials quite rightly pointed out to the assembled workers that they had been contracted for a two-day job and should have finished clearing the runway in that time. The workers contended that it was the officials themselves who had coerced them into attending the rallies, so they were entitled to the extra day on full pay.

It was a standoff and I was aghast. There were still about three hundred metres to clear and time was running out. I spoke to the officials and then through them to the people. There was much angry shouting and at one time, I yelled at a young man who had done little actual work to shut up. The crowd went momentarily quiet and I felt Moffat tugging at my sleeve.

"Leave them to it Boss," He advised quietly. "They are very angry and we could get hurt."

I sourly pointed out that we would be hurt far more if the aeroplane was unable to get us out of there and continued trying to make the workers see sense and get back to work. Eventually they did and by Friday afternoon, the runway was cleared. The surface was pretty rough, but the First Quantum pilot would have just over a thousand metres of free space to land in. Someone had even erected a crudely fashioned windsock so that he or she would be able to choose the best approach.

Moffat must have told Adriano of my dietary preferences and for my last meal in Faina – indeed my last meal in Mozambique - I was given prawns and rice. What a pleasure that was. Mozambique prawns are justly famous for their size and their succulent flavour so I did full justice to the feast.

Saturday dawned sunny and clear for once and by eight o'clock we were all packed and ready to go. The aircraft would be coming from Ndola and would be stopping at Lusaka to pick up members of the Press and at Tete for immigration formalities, so I didn't expect it much before midday. Nevertheless, I was prowling fretfully along the runway some three hours before this. Zeka Jose and Adriano had carried our bags down to the strip for us and I handed out my last stock of fish hooks and needles to thank them for the wonderful care they had given us. My jaundiced opinion of Chinde and its citizens had been alleviated by their kindness and hospitality, but there was still one more shock in store.

Word had obviously gone around that there was an '*ndege*' coming in and the handful of spectators rapidly grew into a sizeable crowd. They were obviously excited at this disruption to dreary daily routine and there was a buzz going around that was almost tangible. A police motor bike drove through the people and came over to me so I braced myself for more trouble.

But it was a young constable on the bike who greeted me politely. Through Adriano I asked him what he wanted and he solemnly informed me that his boss had sent him here in case there were presents being handed out.

Without raising my voice or showing any sign of my inner feelings, I told him to remind his boss that I had already told him that he was a disgrace to his uniform and he was not getting anything from me.

The constable rode away without comment and I wondered what message he would actually pass on.

Shortly after twelve, the aircraft came into view. A Cessna Caravan twelve-seater, it came in low over the runway then shot

193

back into the sky, did a wide circle and came in again from the opposite direction. I could feel emotion welling in my chest as it bumped over the ground towards us and I walked slowly out from the gathered throng to meet it.

First out was my wonderful sponsor, Andy Taylor the Managing Director of Cowbell. He held out his hand and I burst into tears for the umpteenth time.

"Cry Mr Lemon," He said quietly. "You deserve it."

Photographers and cameramen poured out of the aircraft and for a while there was pandemonium as the First Quantum representative Bruce Lewis distributed caps and black tee shirts inscribed with the FQM logo and the words, 'The David Lemon Walk' among the assembled visitors. Breaking off from the questioning media, I appropriated a few samples for my friends at Faina Village then went back to the grilling. It was all very good natured and I kept my emotions in check but when I posed for the very last photograph between Moffat and Zaire, I was very weepy indeed.

An hour after she had brought the aircraft down, chief pilot, Claire Burdett – I had known her as a child in Zimbabwe – wheeled the machine around and roared off into the wind. The wheels lifted from the ground and Andy pushed a cold beer into my hand.

I was going home.

REFLECTIONS

It is barely two years since I completed my walk down the length of the Zambezi but it feels like part of another life. I knew when I finished the walk that I had achieved something very special, but it all took many months to accept in my own mind.

Staring out of the window of the First Quantum aircraft on the return flight to Ndola, I looked down at that mighty river and marvelled that any person could walk through those swamps and forests. From above it did not appear possible and I struggled to believe that I had just done it myself.

I said my good byes to Moffat and Isiah at Tete airport. Mawaya as always, was late picking them up and I didn't get a chance to thank him personally for all he had put into my trip. Although he always brushed off my expressions of gratitude, I knew that without his assistance so freely and generously offered, I probably would not have survived the walk.

Airborne again, I peered down at the Zambian countryside and felt sad that I would be leaving it behind. Beneath that vast mat of vegetation, there were tracks and paths linking villages, there were people leading simple lives in the bush and there were wild animals that were part of my African heritage. Not too many wild animals it was true, but I remembered the scraggy lion in the Lower Zambezi Park and smiled to myself. Although I hadn't seen them, there would have been other lions around and thanks to the dedication of people like Ian Stephenson of CLZ and his protégées like Jacob Katiyo, they still have a chance of ultimate survival as a species.

In Mozambique, the only wild life I had seen had been in the forests around Mphingwe Lodge. Wherever I went, I passed signs warning of elephants yet no trace of any elephants had I seen. That was sad, but Chief Inyambo Yeta had assured me that the Peace Parks Foundation were doing their best to get wild life flourishing again in the country. It will take education as well as money, but if the few dedicated individuals who are doing so much could only be supported by national governments, there is still a chance for African wild life.

Back in Ndola I was greeted by a handful of people and once

again, struggled to keep the tears in check. Darkness was sweeping across the countryside and sitting on Andy Taylor's veranda that evening, I felt the tension of months on the road slowly ebbing from my shoulders. It was over. I could relax and take each day as it came without worrying about getting kilometres behind me or reaching a particular point.

It really was a heady feeling and I slept well that night.

I had a wonderful few weeks in Zambia. I stayed at beautifully peaceful Cherry Farm outside Ndola for most of the time, but I also gave talks and conservation lectures to schools and organisations in towns as far afield as Solwezi and Lusaka. I spent hours being interviewed by various media organisations and generally enjoyed being a minor celebrity.

I had not escaped the Zambezi unscathed however. My feet were very painful and a number of hard black lumps appeared and started growing on my toes and heels. I had no idea what they were but eventually, Shelagh Brown dug six circular creatures out of my feet and these were identified in the local hospital as chioga fleas. I remembered rather too late the warning given to me by Vita about *skelms* in the sand at Chinde.

Shelagh's ministrations were painful, but once the little creatures were out, my health seemed to improve dramatically and life in the little Zambian town of Ndola was fun. When I walked around, people would stop me and ask if they could have their photograph taken with me, so it was all very enjoyable. Gradually I began to regain my lost weight and eventually I began to enjoy the attention I was receiving. My ego was flattered I suppose, but I knew that all too soon I would have to resume 'normal' life and get back to work.

Back in Britain, I settled down to write this book, but for months I couldn't concentrate. I knew what I wanted to say but couldn't formulate the words and my frustration increased by the day.

When my ankles began swelling up, I panicked. Months previously I had passed through an area where a number of villagers suffered from elephantiasis or lymphatic filariasis, which leads to grotesque swelling of the limbs and other parts of the body. I didn't want that and eventually ended up under the care of a lovely Spanish consultant from the tropical diseases department at Southmead hospital in Bristol.

Having told Begonia Bovill all about my trip and shown her my swollen legs, she ordered the taking of a load of my blood and when the results came back, it seemed that I carried an army of bugs in my system. The already grotesque and blackened swellings were discovered to be a side effect of a blood pressure tablet, but I had bilharzia bugs, strongoloides and hydatid worms swimming around inside me. I also had trypanosomes which lead to sleeping sickness and that worried me, not so much for the disease as for the cure which I had been told was most unpleasant.

The tests also revealed that at some stage in the preceding year or so, I had suffered from tick typhus, a debilitating disease that really flattens the sufferer. I could only wonder which particular period of feeling dreadful had been due to that little nasty.

My inability to concentrate was put down to 'brain scarring' following the cerebral malaria. Dr Bovill assured me that it would clear in time and it has.

It took months before I could finally accept the enormity of what I had achieved and even now, it seems slightly unreal. After all, no geriatric (and I was less than three months short of my seventieth birthday when I completed the walk) should be able to walk over three thousand kilometres through wild African countryside.

But I had and it was only when I read words written by Mike Boon who was the first man to kayak the length of the Zambezi that I began to accept and realise just what I had achieved. Mike had obviously suffered from the same feelings of unreality after his epic journey and commented that it is not important that people know or understand about one's achievements. What matters is acknowledging them to oneself and accepting that one has done well.

I knew I had done pretty well for an old toppie and as the chapters unrolled in my narrative, memories of people, places and events flooded back. Most of the memories were good ones and aided by the notes I had kept during the journey this book gradually took shape. I knew that I was probably fortunate to have survived the walk and almost certainly would not have, had it not been for the kindness of people I had met along the way.

I was fortunate too in my sponsors. Andy Taylor and his Cowbell team were always there when I needed them and Sean Whittome allowed the First Quantum Minerals aeroplane to fly in to Chinde and bring me back when it was all over. Further afield, Tom Naude and his crew at Fluxcon in Pretoria loaned me the satellite telephone that in the hands of Mawaya and Ronnie saved my life when cerebral malaria laid me low.

And of course there were so many others who had helped in one way or another. The memories of their willing assistance and genuine kindness will never fade and while I have only been able to mention a few, I hope that those I have missed out will read my story and remember the skinny old chap who walked amongst them and shared their lives ever so briefly.

Now it is done. The journey is over but there have to be other challenges to see me through my dotage. There will be more discomfort, more pain and more exhaustion somewhere in Africa, but there will be so many compensations. I will again have the freedom to do exactly as I like and will witness more spectacular sunsets and listen to dawn choruses that soothe my soul. I will walk among the elephants, the noisy impala and the hippopotami again and I will enjoy the star-filled skies that only Africa can provide. I will mix with beautiful people and try to share their lives as closely as I can. I will see sights that are only available to the solitary wanderer and I will survive again. Although I know in my heart that it all has to end at some stage, I feel that I am still young enough and fit enough to undertake more adventures.

Mind you, I am not at all sure that anything will be able to match the excitement, the effort or the challenge of walking the length of the Mighty Zambezi.

POSTSCRIPT

Although the pair of them were responsible for saving my life when cerebral malaria almost killed me, those two wonderful men who accompanied me down the 'Livingstone Trail' have both passed on since I completed my walk.

Ronnie Henwood, that quietly cheerful little man with an encyclopaedic knowledge of David Livingstone's travels succumbed to cancer in September 2015.

In April 2016 Johan Mawaya Hougaard took his own life, leaving me saddened and desperately upset at the loss of two men who had not only kept me alive, but had become true friends over a very short period of time.

I can only hope that I can enjoy further adventures with the pair of them when I also enter that heavenly bushveld.

THE END

GLOSSARY

Banana Boat: Canoe-like vessel made from wood or fibreglass and propelled by paddles or a small outboard motor.

Barbel: African catfish from the genus *barbus*.

Biltong: Spicy dried meat, similar to American jerky.

Boma: Protective enclosure made with thorn branches.

Bom Dia: Portuguese greeting – literally Good Day.

Boomslang: *Dispholidus typus* - a large, venomous snake in the family Colubridae. Literally 'tree snake' in Afrikaans.

Bream: Indigenous fish of the *tilapia* family.

Bundu bashing: Forcing one's way through rough countryside.

Calabash: African name for a gourd.

Chitenge: Wrap around garment worn by both genders.

Kapenta: *Limnothrissa Miodan* – Tanzanian sardine, introduced to Lake Kariba in 1967.

Kays: Local abbreviation for kilometres.

Kwacha: Monetary unit of Zambia.

Lozi: People of Western Zambia, formerly Barotseland.

Madala: Old man.

Massawa: *Uapaca kirkiana* - fruit from a plant found through much of Central Africa. Known as Musuku in other African countries.

Mealies: Maize or corn on the cob. From the Afrikaanz word *mielie*.

Mealie meal: Maize porridge.

Meticais: Plural of *metical* – the monetary unit of Mozambique.

Mopani: *Colosphermum mopane* – a hardwood tree that grows in hot, dry, low-lying areas and only in Africa.

Msasa: *Brachystegia spiciformis* – a medium sized African tree with compound leaves and racemes of small, fragrant green flowers.

Mzungu: White person in many African languages.

Ndege: Literally a bird, but also used to describe aeroplanes.

Nduna: Minor chief or headman.

Njinga: Bicycle.

Nshima: A stodgy maize porridge that is the staple diet of Africa. Ncima in Mozambique and Sadza in Zimbabwe..

Obrigardo: Thank you in Portuguese.

Paw paw: Papaya.

Rondavel: A small round building, usually used as a bedroom.

Scotch Cart: A two wheeled wooden cart, drawn by donkeys or oxen.

Sekuru: Grandfather.

Shumba: Lion in most indigenous languages of Southern Africa.

Sitimbe Tree: A type of Leadwood *(combretum imberbe)* found in Mozambique.

Skelm: A devil or irritating creature.

Tarven: Colloquial name for a Zambian tavern or beer hall.

Tiger fish: *Hydrocynus vittatus* – freshwater fish armed with formidable teeth and famous among anglers for its fighting qualities.

Vlei: A shallow depression in the ground that is often wet.

Wag n'bietjie: Afrikaanz name for *Acacia Caffra* – a cruelly hooked thorn on a small, creeper-like bush.

Wazungu: Plural of *mzungu* – white people.

17203077R00139

Printed in Poland
by Amazon Fulfillment
Poland Sp. z o.o., Wrocław